THE SHAPES AND SOUNDS
OF THE LAO LANGUAGE

The Shapes and Sounds of the
LAO LANGUAGE
For Native English Speakers

DAVID DALE

Orchid Press

THE SHAPES AND SOUNDS OF THE LAO LANGUAGE
David Dale

First edition published privately, Vientiane 2003
Second edition, Orchid Press, Bangkok 2014, 2018

ORCHID PRESS
P.O. Box 19,
Yuttitham Post Office,
Bangkok 10907, Thailand
www.orchidbooks.com

Copyright © David Dale, 2003, 2014, 2018

Protected by copyright under the terms of the International Copyright Union: all rights reserved. Except for fair use in book reviews, no part of this publication may be reproduced in any form or by any means, electronic or mechanical, including photocopying, recording, or by any information storage or retrieval system without prior permission in writing from the copyright holders.

ISBN: 978-974-524-214-2

CONTENTS

Introduction	vii
Downloading Audio Files	viii
Acknowledgements	ix
Definition of Terms	xi

1. Consonants 1
   1.1 Lao Alphabet 1
   1.2 Animals/Objects 1
   1.3 Flash Cards 3
   1.4 Writing 3
   1.5 Consonant Pronunciation 5
   1.6 Pronunciation Tricks 9
      1.6.1 Aspirated and Unaspirated Consonants 9
      1.6.2 The Beginning ງ "ng" 9
   1.7 Final Consonants 10
      1.7.1 Final Stops 10
      1.7.2 Final Nasals 11
      1.7.3 Final Semi-Vowels 12
   1.8 Special ວ Case 12
   1.9 Other Symbols 13
      1.9.1 Lao Numbers 13
      1.9.2 Various Symbols 14
      1.9.3 The Repeat Symbol ๆ 15
2. Vowels 17
   2.1 Lao Vowels 17
      2.1.1 Standard Vowels 17
      2.1.2 Special Vowels 18
   2.2 Final Forms 19
   2.3 Mixed Vowels 20
   2.4 Pronunciation Tricks 23
      2.4.1 Short and Long Vowels 23
      2.4.2 Difficult Vowels 24
      2.4.3 The "a" Sound 26
      2.4.4. The "i" Sound 27
   2.5 Recognition Tricks 27
   2.6 Flash Cards 27

2.7 Writing Practice	28
2.8 Spelling	30
2.9 Mai Gkan and Mai Gkong	31
3. Tones	33
3.1 The Importance of Tones	33
3.2 The Six Basic Tones	34
3.3 Tones 7 and 8	38
3.4 Special Tone Mai Tī	40
3.5 Pronouncing Tones on Short Vowels	41
3.6 Tones on Final Particles	42
3.7 Tone Variations	44
3.8 Tones in Sentences	45
4. Learning the Tones	47
5. Tone Rules	53
5.1 Consonant Classes	53
5.2 Final Stops	56
5.3 Tone Marks	57
5.4 Tone Chart	59
5.5 Tone Mark Placement	61
5.6 Recognizing Tones	62
Answer Key	64
6. Memorization Tricks	67
6.1 Alphabet Memorization Trick	67
6.2 Consonant Class Memorization Trick	67
7. Accompanying Audio Text	69
7.1 Chapter 1 Associated Text	69
7.2 Chapter 2 Associated Text	75
7.3 Chapter 3 Associated Text	79
7.4 Chapter 4 Associated Text	83
7.5 Chapter 5 Associated Text	86
7.6 Graded Reading and Listening Material	88
7.7 Short Stories	114
About the Author	137

INTRODUCTION

The Shapes and Sounds of the Lao Language developed out of materials put together to assist native English speakers living and working in the Lao P.D.R. Both text and audio files were originally assembled for personal language study. Later it seemed apparent that this material would be beneficial to other Lao language learners.

The text before you is not a linguistic treatise or comprehensive analysis of the Lao language from a scientific perspective. Rather, it is written as a practical guide with the native English speaker in mind. It focuses on approaches that will help the native English speaker understand how to read, write and pronounce the Lao language. There is a special emphasis on learning to distinguish and pronounce the Lao tones.

This text does not teach grammar, vocabulary, syntax or parts of speech. Consequently, the Lao language learner will need more than this volume alone. A repertoire of materials is recommended so the Lao language learner will have exposure to many approaches and aspects of the language.

Perhaps the most useful feature of this work is the accompanying audio files. The audio follows the examples given in the text and allows the reader to hear a native speaker pronounce what they are reading. The advantage of using digital audio files is that the language learner can immediately jump to whichever part he or she wishes to practice. You will notice large gray numbers next to Lao examples in the text. These correspond with the track number of the accompanying audio where you can listen to that example. Also, the last chapter of the book contains the complete text that is in the audio files in sequential order.

Speaking, reading and writing Lao is very rewarding! You will find it very difficult at times to wrap your tongue around some of the strange sounds, and at times you may find the tones impossible. But with some time and diligence you will make progress and be satisfied. This text is offered in hope that it may assist you on your journey.

DOWNLOADING ACCOMPANYING AUDIO FILES

To download the MP3 format audio files that are designed to accompany this text, please enter into your browser the following URL:

       http://www.orchidbooks.com/audio/index.html

You will be requested to enter your name, a valid Email address and a password.

       The password for this download is `ht$G54x`

The download will consist of a compressed folder. UnZIP the folder to locate the audio files within. These files may then be played on any current MP3 compatible device or on your computer.

If there are any difficulties downloading or using the audio files, please contact Orchid Press for further assistance, at <downloadhelp@orchidbooks.com>

ACKNOWLEDGEMENTS

Without the help and encouragement of many people I would not have been able to put this book together. There are many people who contributed and who should be acknowledged:

Ben Shue and Sun Seng were the first people who asked me to share with them some of the things I had been learning regarding the Lao pronunciation and tones. Preparing for those sessions led to the assembling of much of the material in this book.

Kaeva Saepharn donated many hours typing portions of the Lao text and helping to proof-read the final text.

ARDA English School in Vientiane, Lao P.D.R. graciously provided a place for me to do the recordings for the accompanying audio files.

Pamela Sue Wright introduced me to the tone contour recording computer program. Much of the work in this book is based on the information gathered with that program. Also, Ms. Wright helped give valuable linguistic insight for the writing of this book.

More than anyone, Somphet Phomavongsa, a professor at the National University of Laos and my personal tutor, deserves credit and acknowledgement. He was the first person to successfully teach Lao tones to me. All of the Lao language recordings on the accompanying audio files are Professor Phomavongsa's voice. He also helped me by proof-reading the Lao language sections in the written text. His assistance has been invaluable!

There are many others who previewed early samples of this book and gave encouragement and suggestions. I appreciate everyone's help.

I offer this book with hopes that it will be useful for expatriates who come to work in Laos as they attempt to learn the Lao language, and in doing so come close to the heart of the Lao people.

David Dale
Vientiane, Lao P.D.R.
2003

DEFINITION OF TERMS

Some of the terms you will encounter in the following text may be new to you. In most places a simple definition for terms is given as they appear in the text. Here is a list to assist you with some terms that may need a little more definition.

Aspiration—Refers to the pronunciation of a consonant with a good puff of air like the "p" in the English work "pit".

Consonant Class—Lao has three consonant "classes" or categories - High, Middle and Low. The class of a consonant is one element in determining the tone of a Lao word, but the name of the class does not describe the tone of the consonant.

Dialect—A regional version of a language that is distinguished by its unique accent, set of tone and special terms. A dialect, though different, is mutually intelligible with the wider language.

Glottal Stop—A glottal stop is produced by closing the air passage way at the very back of the mouth to stop or begin a sound. A glottal stop in Lao occurs when the vowel sound is abruptly cut off without the aid of a final consonant.

Luang Prabang—The old royal capital of Laos, north of the present day capital Vientiane. The dialect of Luang Prabang is noted for the high pronunciation of the High Class Consonants.

Nasal—A nasal consonant is one in which the sound is partially produced in the nasal cavity, such as "m" and "n" in English.

Orthography—refers to the system of writing, or script, of a language.

Rounding—Refers to the shape of the mouth during the pronunciation of a vowel. A "rounded" vowel, like the English "o", is produced by positioning your lips in a round shape. Conversely, for an "unrounded" vowel, like the English "e", the lips are "flat".

Stop—A stop is an abrupt end to the sound of a word or syllable.

Tone—Refers to the pitch and contour of a word or syllable.

Transliteration—Using one script to write the sound of another.
Vientiane—The capital of Laos and the home of the "standard" dialect.
Vowel Length—The length of time the vowel sound is pronounced.

1
CONSONANTS

1.1 Lao Alphabet

T 01

ກ ຂ ຄ ງ ຈ ສ ຊ ຍ ດ ຕ ຖ ທ ນ ບ ປ ຜ ຝ ພ
ຟ ມ ຍ ລ ວ ຫ ອ ຮ

In Lao, when you pronounce the name of a consonant, you always use the long vowel "ໍອ" (like the "o" in the word "cost") after the sound of the consonant. The alphabet would then be: gkǭ, khǭ, khǭ, ngǭ, chǭ, sǭ, sǭ, nyǭ, dǭ, dtǭ, thǭ, thǭ, nǭ, bǭ, bpǭ, phǭ, fǭ, phǭ, fǭ, mǭ, yǭ, lǭ, vǭ, hǭ, ǭ, hǭ. (The reason it appears that some are repeated is because they have different tonal values. You'll learn more about that later.)

Though it may seem like a daunting task, you can successfully learn the Lao script! Don't be intimidated by the fact that it bears no similarity to English. Once you learn it you will be surprised at how easy it was! And all Lao people will be very impressed with you when you are able to read and write the script.

1.2 Animals/Objects

When the Lao alphabet is taught to Lao children they learn each letter of the alphabet along with a word that begins with that letter. This helps them in remembering the alphabet. It is also useful to learn these words, which are mostly animals and objects. It helps in Lao conversation if you are trying to figure out the correct pronunciation of a word, or which letter the Lao speaker is using when saying a word you are trying to understand. *Is that "b" as in "bāe" (goat), or is that "bp" as in "bpā" (fish)?* Even if you don't pronounce the consonants absolutely correct, the Lao speaker will

1

Shapes and Sounds

know which one you are talking about by the name of the animal, since virtually all Lao people are familiar with the standard animals/objects associated with each consonant. Here are the animals/objects for the Lao consonants (the numbers correspond to the tones for the words, which you'll learn later):

T 02

ກ	ໄກ່	gk	gkai (2)	chicken
ຂ	ໄຂ່	kh	khai (2)	egg
ຄ	ຄວາຍ	kh	khwāi (3)	buffalo
ງ	ງົວ	ng	ngōua (3)	cow
ຈ	ຈອກ	ch	chǫk (6)	cup
ສ	ເສືອ	s	sēua (4)	tiger
ຊ	ຊ້າງ	s	sāng (5)	elephant
ຍ	ຍຸງ	ny	nyoung (3)	mosquito
ດ	ເດັກ	d	dek (7)	child
ຕ	ຕາ	dt	dtā (1)	eyes
ຖ	ຖົງ	th	thong (4)	bag
ທ	ທຸງ	th	thoung (3)	flag
ນ	ນົກ	n	nok (8)	bird
ບ	ແບ້	b	bāe (5)	goat
ປ	ປາ	bp	bpā (1)	fish
ຜ	ເຜິ້ງ	ph	phueng (6)	bee
ຝ	ຝົນ	f	fon (4)	rain
ພ	ພູ	ph	phōu (3)	mountain
ຟ	ໄຟ	f	fai (3)	fire
ມ	ແມວ	m	māeo (3)	cat
ຍ	ຍາ	y	yā (1)	medicine
ລ	ລິງ	l	līng (3)	monkey

Shapes and Sounds

ວ	ວີ	v	vī (3)	fan
ຫ	ຫ່ານ	h	hān (2)	goose
ອ	ໂອ	silent	ō (1)	bowl *
ຮ	ເຮືອນ	h	hēuan (3)	house

* The ອ is used as a silent consonant to "hold" the vowel for words that begin with a vowel sound. It is also used as a vowel in some situations, which you will learn later.

1.3 Flash Cards

More important than learning the order of the consonants in the alphabet is being able to recognize them on sight. A good way to practice Lao consonants is to make flash cards, each with one consonant on the front, and the transliteration on the back. Spend some time trying to memorize them and test yourself. Mix the order up and try again. After you have done this several times, remove the easiest one from the stack and start over. If you find you are always confusing a few consonants, pull them out and take special note of the differences in the way they are written. As you know, several of the consonants appear to be repeated. That is because they have different tonal values, but the same consonant sound. For now, don't worry about the tone but just remember the consonant sound that goes with it. We will get to tones later. If you do this well within one or two days you will have all the Lao consonants memorized and be able to recognize each one when you see it.

1.4 Writing

When you write the Lao consonants (or other marks) you always begin at the "head" of the consonant. The "head" is the little circle that appears on each consonant. As with English, native speakers and writers will write the letters less "perfect" than the printed version. First, learn to write the consonants according to the idealized form. Later, look at the more "relaxed" version of writing the consonants and become comfortable in your own style. (Also, remember that if

Shapes and Sounds

you want to become proficient in Lao such that you can write like a native speaker, then don't worry about "abandoning" the idealized form in order to write Lao like most Lao people's handwriting. If your writing follows the idealized print too closely it will look "too perfect" for native speakers and, though they will say it is beautiful, it will look like a child or a foreigner wrote it. For example, most of the "heads" of consonants aren't drawn in native Lao people's handwriting. But to be sure you don't abandon the wrong elements, look at how a native Lao writes.)

Practice writing the consonants by tracing them below. Remember to begin at the "head" of the consonant:

ກ ຂ ຄ ງ ຈ ສ ຊ ຍ ດ ຕ ຖ ທ ນ ບ
ປ ຜ ຝ ພ ຟ ມ ຢ ລ ວ ຫ ອ ຮ

ກ ຂ ຄ ງ ຈ ສ ຊ ຍ ດ ຕ ຖ ທ ນ ບ
ປ ຜ ຝ ພ ຟ ມ ຢ ລ ວ ຫ ອ ຮ

ກ ຂ ຄ ງ ຈ ສ ຊ ຍ ດ ຕ ຖ ທ ນ ບ
ປ ຜ ຝ ພ ຟ ມ ຢ ລ ວ ຫ ອ ຮ

ກ ຂ ຄ ງ ຈ ສ ຊ ຍ ດ ຕ ຖ ທ ນ ບ
ປ ຜ ຝ ພ ຟ ມ ຢ ລ ວ ຫ ອ ຮ

ກ ຂ ຄ ງ ຈ ສ ຊ ຍ ດ ຕ ຖ ທ ນ ບ
ປ ຜ ຝ ພ ຟ ມ ຢ ລ ວ ຫ ອ ຮ

ກ ຂ ຄ ງ ຈ ສ ຊ ຍ ດ ຕ ຖ ທ ນ ບ
ປ ຜ ຝ ພ ຟ ມ ຢ ລ ວ ຫ ອ ຮ

Now, practice a more "relaxed" form of writing the Lao consonants:

ກ ຂ ຄ ງ ຈ ສ ຊ ຍ ດ ຕ ຖ ທ ນ ບ
ປ ຜ ຝ ພ ຟ ມ ຢ ຣ ລ ວ ຫ ອ ຮ

ກ ຂ ຄ ງ ຈ ສ ຊ ຍ ດ ຕ ຖ ທ ນ ບ
ປ ຜ ຝ ພ ຟ ມ ຢ ຣ ລ ວ ຫ ອ ຮ

ກ ຂ ຄ ງ ຈ ສ ຊ ຍ ດ ຕ ຖ ທ ນ ບ
ປ ຜ ຝ ພ ຟ ມ ຢ ຣ ລ ວ ຫ ອ ຮ

ກ ຂ ຄ ງ ຈ ສ ຊ ຍ ດ ຕ ຖ ທ ນ ບ
ປ ຜ ຝ ພ ຟ ມ ຢ ຣ ລ ວ ຫ ອ ຮ

ກ ຂ ຄ ງ ຈ ສ ຊ ຍ ດ ຕ ຖ ທ ນ ບ
ປ ຜ ຝ ພ ຟ ມ ຢ ຣ ລ ວ ຫ ອ ຮ

ກ ຂ ຄ ງ ຈ ສ ຊ ຍ ດ ຕ ຖ ທ ນ ບ
ປ ຜ ຝ ພ ຟ ມ ຢ ຣ ລ ວ ຫ ອ ຮ

1.5 Consonant Pronunciation

ກ This is pronounced like the "k" in the word "skate". Most people transliterate this as "g" but it is actually an unaspirated "k" sound. Since there is not a regular "g" consonant in Lao you can get away with this. In this book ກ is transliterated as "gk"

ຂ This is pronounced like the "k" in the word "kite". It is aspirated and is therefore typically transliterated as "kh". The only difference between ຂ and the next one, ຄ, is that ຂ has a rising tone and ຄ has a high tone.

ຄ This is pronounced like the "k" in the word "kite". It is aspirated and is therefore typically transliterated as "kh".

Shapes and Sounds

ງ This is pronounced like the "ng" in the word "sing". However, unlike English, it is often found at the beginning of a word.

ຈ This consonant is typically transliterated with either "j" or "ch" but its sound is actually somewhere in between. The ຈ has a little more of an abrupt sound than the English "j" and not as much aspiration as the English "ch". It is unvoiced and unaspirated. In this book ຈ is transliterated as "ch".

ສ This is pronounced like the "s" in the word "see". It is transliterated as "s". The only difference between ສ and the next one, ຊ, is that ສ has a rising tone and ຊ has a high tone.

ຊ This is pronounced like the "s" in the word "see". It is transliterated as "s" or "x". It is transliterated as "x" in some systems where "s" is then reserved for ສ. However, in this book ຊ is transliterated as "s".

ຍ This is pronounced like the "ny" in the word "canyon". Like ງ, ຍ is often found at the beginning of a word (as opposed to English where the "ny" sound cannot appear at the beginning of a word). As in this book, it is usually transliterated as "ny" though formerly it was often transliterated as "nj" or "gn".

ດ This is pronounced like the "d" in the word "dog". It is typically transliterated as "d".

ຕ This is pronounced like the "t" in the word "stop". It is somewhere between "d" and "t" as we know them in English. Unlike a beginning "t" in English, ຕ is unaspirated. However, unlike "d" in English, ຕ is unvoiced. Though this sound exists in English (when a "t" immediately follows another consonant), in Lao it can appear by itself at the beginning of a word or syllable. Therefore it is important not to confuse it with ດ or ທ/ຖ. This is usually transliterated as "t" or "dt", as in this book.

ຖ This is pronounced like the "t" in the word "tape". It is aspirated and is therefore typically transliterated as "th" but it should not be pronounced like the "th" in English. The only difference between ຖ and the next one, ທ, is that ຖ has a rising tone and ທ has a high tone.

Shapes and Sounds

ຕ   This is pronounced like the "t" in the word "tape". It is aspirated and is therefore typically transliterated as "th" but it should not be pronounced like the "th" in English.

ນ   This is pronounced like the "n" in the word "name". It is typically transliterated as "n".

ບ   This is pronounced like the "b" in the word "boy". It is typically transliterated as "b".

ປ   This is pronounced like the "p" in the word "spit". It is somewhere between "b" and "p" as we know them in English. Unlike a beginning "p" in English, ປ is unaspirated. However, unlike "b" in English, ປ is unvoiced. Though this sound exists in English (when a "p" immediately follows another consonant), in Lao it can appear by itself at the beginning of a word or syllable. Therefore it is important not to confuse it with ບ or ຜ/ພ. This is usually transliterated as "p" or "bp", as in this book.

ຜ   This is pronounced like the "p" in the word "pit". It is aspirated and is therefore typically transliterated as "ph" but it should not be pronounced like the "ph" in English. The only difference between ຜ and ພ, is that ຜ has a rising tone and ພ has a high tone.

ຝ   This is pronounced like the "f" in the word "face". It is typically transliterated as "f". The only difference between ຝ and ຟ, is that ຝ has a rising tone and ຟ has a high tone.

ພ   This is pronounced like the "p" in the word "pit". It is aspirated and is therefore typically transliterated as "ph" but it should not be pronounced like the "ph" in English.

ຟ   This is pronounced like the "f" in the word "face". It is typically transliterated as "f".

ມ   This is pronounced like the "m" in the word "mouse". It is typically transliterated as "m".

ຢ   This is pronounced like the "y" in the word "yellow". It is typically transliterated as "y".

7

Shapes and Sounds

(ຣ) This consonant used to appear in the Lao alphabet here and some are beginning to include it again. It is pronounced like the letter "r" and is mostly found in old and royal language. At times the ຣ is "flapped" like the common "r" in Spanish and often trilled. The ຣ is also occasionally found as the second letter of a double consonant. In modern Lao this is most often dropped out, though you still see it from time to time. In places where ຣ would stand on its own you currently find ລ in its place. (Examples of words with ຣ are found in Track 03 in the accompanying audio files. **T 03**)

ລ This is pronounced like the "l" in the word "land". It is typically transliterated as "l".

ວ This consonant is pronounced as either "v" as in the word "van", or "w" as in the word "way". You will hear some native speakers pronounce it more one way than the other, and vice versa. The Lao do not make a distinction between these two sounds, as we do in English, so you can get away with doing either. It appears that ວ is closer to "v" more often than "w".

ຫ This is pronounced like the "h" in the word "hand" with nasalization. It is typically transliterated as "h". The only difference between ຫ and ຮ, is that ຫ has a rising tone and ຮ has a high tone.

ອ This symbol (also used for a vowel in some circumstances) is used for a silent consonant and serves as a "vowel holder" for words or syllables that begin with a vowel sound. Linguistically, it can be considered a beginning glottal stop, but for all practical purposes just consider it a silent consonant.

ຮ This is pronounced like the "h" in the word "hand" with nasalization. It is typically transliterated as "h".

1.6 Pronunciation Tricks

1.6.1 Aspirated and Unaspirated Consonants

Unaspirated Consonants		Aspirated Consonants	
mid class (low tones)		high class (rising tone)	low class (high tone)
soft (voiced)	abrupt (unvoiced)		
- (g) gate	ກ (k / gk) skate	ຂ (kh) Kate	ຄ (kh) Kate
ດ (d) Dan	ຕ (t / dt) Stan	ຖ (th) tan	ທ (th) tan
ບ (b) bit	ປ (p / bp) spit	ຜ (ph) pit	ພ (ph) pit

Special attention should be given to the consonants in the second column: ກ, ຕ, and ປ. These consonant sounds only occur in English when they immediately follow another consonant sound. The difference in pronunciation between the first and second columns is real (that is, they do have different sounds) and sometimes words differ in meaning by this slight pronunciation difference. (Practice examples of the aspirated and unaspirated consonants are found in Track 04 - 06 of the accompanying audio. **T 04-07**)

Consonant ຈ: The correct pronunciation of ຈ would place it in the second column with ກ, ຕ, and ປ. The English "j" would be in the first column with g, d, and b, and the English "ch" would be in the third or fourth columns with kh, th, and ph. (Practice examples of words with ຈ are found in Track 07 of the accompanying audio. **T 07**)

1.6.2 The Beginning ງ "ng"

The Lao consonant ງ ("ng") is often found at the beginning of words and syllables. In English it only occurs at the end of syllables. Consequently, native English speakers may find ງ difficult to pronounce in such situations. A common mistake is to pronounce it like "n" or like "g" since it is often transliterated "ng". But it is best just to consider ງ its own sound and not try to pronounce two sounds at the same time. Below is a trick for training your tongue and mouth to be able to produce the beginning ງ sound. Take heart! You can certainly master this sound, and with some

Shapes and Sounds

practice you will be able to fluently pronounce it without even having to think about it!

Take the English word "sing". You shouldn't have any problem pronouncing that. Then add a sound on to the end of it. Let's add the syllable "-ām" which rhymes with "mom" (American English). That gives us the word "singām". Can you pronounce that? Try to say it without any break in the sound. (If it is difficult to say without a break, think of the word "singer" in English and how you normally say that without a break in the sound, and then try to do the same with "singām.") Now take off the beginning "s". This gives us the word "ingām". Practice pronouncing this word many times. It should still have two syllables, but the sound should be continuous. No problem! Right? Now begin to whisper the "i" sound at the beginning and then continue to pronounce the rest of the word normally. Make sure you don't whisper the "ng" sound. Try to memorize the position of your tongue in your mouth as you pronounce this word. Slowly, after hundreds of repetitions, drop the "i" sound altogether to leave you with a one syllable word "ngām". Can you do it? Congratulations! You are now saying "beautiful" in Lao: ງາມ. You can try this with other words and syllables as you please.

sing
singer
singām
ingām
(i)ngām
ngām

(Practice examples of words that begin with ງ are found in Track 08 of the accompanying audio. **T 08**)

1.7 Final Consonants

Lao has 8 final consonants: ກ ດ ບ ງ ນ ມ ຍ ວ In actuality, there are 6 final consonant sounds; the remaining two are vowel sounds and are called "semi-vowels".

1.7.1 Final Stops

A final stop is an abrupt end to the sound of a word or syllable. An example is the "t" in the English word "night". There are actually four final stops in Lao, three of which are written as consonants. The three consonants are ກ ດ ບ. In the initial positions these consonants would be pronounced as ກ: "gk", ດ: "d" ບ: "b". However, in the final position they are pronounced as ກ: "k", ດ: "t" ບ: "p". This is important to remember. If you pronounce them as a final "g", "d", or "b" they will not sound correct.

Also, be careful not to aspirate the final stop. For example, in the English word "night" the final "t" is a final stop and is unaspirated. However, it is common practice for English speakers to aspirate the final "t" when attempting to pronounce the word clearly for another person to understand. In normal English speaking, however, the "t" in "night" is unaspirated and serves as a final stop. This "normal" pronunciation of the final "t" is how the final ດ in Lao should be spoken. The same is true of ກ and ບ. (Examples of final stops are found in Track 09 of the accompanying audio. T 09)

The fourth final stop in Lao is a glottal stop. A glottal stop is when the vowel sound is abruptly cut off without the aid of a final consonant. This is comparatively rare in English, though not uncommon in spoken English. (An example of a glottal stop in English is on the first syllable of the expression "Uh-oh!"—said when something is found to be wrong.)

The glottal stop is not written in Lao. It only occurs when there is a short vowel without a final consonant. We will discuss Lao vowels below. After you learn them you will be able to recognize the presence of a glottal stop. It is important because final stops, including the glottal stop, affect the tonal value of a word in Lao. (Four of the eight Lao tones cannot occur with a final stop.)

1.7.2 Final Nasals

A nasal consonant is one in which the sound is partially produced in the nasal cavity. Lao has three final nasal consonants: ງ ນ ມ. That is "ng", "n" and "m" respectively. All of these sounds occur in English so pronouncing them should not present a great difficulty. The important thing to note is that the presence of final nasals does not affect the tones of Lao words. Tones are pronounced *through* the final nasal consonant, particularly, in words with short vowels. (Examples of words with final nasals are found in Track 10 of the accompanying audio. T 10)

Shapes and Sounds

1.7.3 Final "Semi-Vowels"

Two consonants that often appear in the final position are ຍ and ວ. Although ຍ and ວ in the initial position are consonants and would be pronounced as "ny" and "v" respectively, in the final position they are serving as parts of vowel sounds. Consequently, like the final nasals, they do not affect the tone of the Lao word. We will discuss these types of vowels in the next chapter

1.8 Special ວ Case

The consonant ວ also appears in some words following the initial consonant and preceding the vowel. The ວ is a consonant in this usage and not a vowel. It is pronounced like a "w" in English when joined with the preceding consonant, or like the "u" in English words that begin with "q" such as "queen". So, the word ຂາ ("khā") would become ຂວາ ("khwā" or "quā"). There are a few very common words that contain the special ວ. Here is a sample list below:

T 11

ກວ່າ	gkwā	"more"
ກວາງ	gkwāng	"deer"
ກວາງຂວາງ	gkwāng	"large"
ແຂວງ	khwāeng	"province"
ຄວາຍ	khwāi	"buffalo"
ຄວາມ	khwām	auxiliary word that makes an adjective a noun
ຂວາ	khwā	"right" (opposite of left)

In the next chapter you will learn about Lao vowels. One of the vowels you will learn is the ◌ົວ "ōua". (The X here represents the consonant.) You can see that this vowel contains the ວ symbol. When this vowel is followed by a final consonant, the little mark on the top disappears (That "little mark" is called "mai gkong" and will be discussed later.) For example, ຄົວ ("khōua"—to cook) would become ຄວນ ("khōuan"—should). Here you see the ວ immediately follow the initial consonant, but don't be confused!

This is not the special case of ວ described above because there is no other vowel— ວ is the only vowel here. And the pronunciation, while similar, is a little different.

ຄວນ   Khōuan   ຄວາມ   khwān

At times, even Lao people have a little difficulty pronouncing these words differently, so don't be discouraged if you find this one difficult. (Examples of comparisons of these types of words can be found in Track 12 of the accompanying audio. **T 12**)

1.9 Other Symbols

1.9.1 Lao Numbers

Lao has its own symbols for numbers; however, they are quickly falling out of use. The international Arabic numbers (0, 1, 2, 3, 4, 5, 6, 7, 8, 9) are used generally and many Lao people read the old Lao numeric symbols with difficulty. Nevertheless, you will still encounter them on Lao money, in older publications and occasionally as street numbers. Here are the ten Lao digits with their corresponding Lao name and Arabic number.

T 13

໐	ສູນ	sōun	0
໑	ໜຶ່ງ	neung	1
໒	ສອງ	sǫng	2
໓	ສາມ	sām	3
໔	ສີ່	sī	4
໕	ຫ້າ	hā	5
໖	ຫົກ	hok	6
໗	ເຈັດ	chet	7
໘	ແປດ	bpāet	8
໙	ເກົ້າ	gkao	9
໑໐	ສິບ	sip	10

Shapes and Sounds

As you can see with number ten, Lao digits are assembled the same as Arabic numbers. However, when writing numbers of more than three digits; a period is used, instead of a comma, to separate the parts of the number. This follows the French system. Take care not to confuse this period with a decimal point, which is often represented by a comma instead of a period.

T 15

໑໐໐	໑.໐໐໐	໑໐.໐໐໐	໑໐໐.໐໐໐	໑.໐໐໐.໐໐໐
ຮ້ອຍ	ພັນ	ໝື່ນ	ແສນ	ລ້ານ
100	1,000	10,000	100,000	1,000,000

However, in some cases the system is reversed—commas are used to separate the digits and a period is used for the decimal point. This is becoming more popular as the English speaking world is having more influence on Laos rather than the French. Just be aware that you might see it in one of two ways and you will usually be able to figure it out from the situation.

(More examples of Lao numbers can be found in Tracks 14 and 16 of the accompanying audio. **T 14, T 16**)

1.9.2 Various Symbols

Occasionally you will see a word with a mark under one consonant such as in the word ອິເລັກໂຕຼນິກ (electronic). The ຼ here acts as the consonant ຣ ("r") in such words. (The X represents a consonant.) Usually this occurs in words that come from other languages such as "electronic" or "protein". Later on you will see that the symbol ຼ can also be used for the consonant ລ ("l") when it is transformed into a rising tone. In that case it is written as ຫລ or ຫຼ. Linguistically, "l" and "r" are closely related, so you can understand why this symbol is sometimes used for the "r" sound in double consonants.

Another symbol you will occasionally see is the Mai Garang, X̌. In modern, common Lao this symbol is no longer used. Though it is written similarly to a tone mark, this symbol is used to mark final consonants that were silent. Many Lao words used to have additional final consonants that would indicate the origin of the word, but were unpronounced, and X̌ was placed over these consonants. Now, X̌ is often seen on words that come from other languages which contain final consonants other than the ones that are commonly used in Lao. The is X̌ placed over the final consonant such as ສ໌ ("s") in the word ເອດສ໌ ("AIDS"). More often than not you will see mai garang on signs of foreign businesses in Laos that maintain their company name and transliterate it into the Lao language.

1.9.3 The Repeat Symbol ໆ

It is very common to find words repeated for emphasis in Lao. Instead of writing the word twice, however, Lao uses the repeat symbol: ໆ. Any word this is placed after should be read twice.

ນ້ອຍໆ	nǫi nǫi	"very little"
ທຸກໆ	thouk thouk	"every single…"
ໄປໆ	bpai bpai	"go!"

15

NOTES

2
VOWELS

2.1 Lao Vowels

There are 12 pairs of standard vowels in Lao, each pair consisting of a short and long version of the same vowel sound. All of the short vowels in these pairs are pronounced with a final glottal stop. That means that the sound is abruptly stopped without any consonant sound. There are four "special" vowels in Lao and 30 mixed vowel combinations when standard vowels are joined with one of the two "semi-vowel" endings (ຢ and ວ). However, of those 30 mixed vowels only 12 are commonly used.

Many of the Lao vowels are not equal to English vowels so pay careful attention to the sound and position of the mouth during pronunciation. There are many systems of transliteration for Lao vowels and none of them are perfect. Phonetic symbols do exist for all of the Lao vowel sounds but the average person is not familiar with them. Using symbols or letters that are common to English often misleads the reader as to the true sound of the Lao vowel. Consequently, it is important to learn the Lao script as soon as possible so that you do not have to rely on any system of transliteration. You can do it! It is not as difficult as it may appear at the outset!

The X in the symbols below represents the consonant that would "hold" the vowel.

2.1.1 Standard Vowels

There are the 12 pairs of standard vowels in Lao. The terms "long" and "short" to describe Lao vowels has to do with the length of time the vowel sound is pronounced. The short vowels are spoken very quickly—as short as possible—and then ended with a final glottal stop. An apostrophe is used to indicate the final glottal stop in the transliteration. The long vowels have the same sound, but they are

17

Shapes and Sounds

pronounced for a longer period of time and are not stopped. The small horizontal lines over the vowels in the transliteration indicate they are long vowels. Long vowels end with a natural "fade" rather than the abrupt stop of the short vowels. The last three pairs of vowels in the list below are dipthongs.

T 17

SHORT		LONG	
Xະ	a'	Xາ	ā
◌ิX	i'	◌ีX	ī
◌ึX	eu'	◌ืX	ēu
Xุ	ou'	Xู	ōu
ເXະ	e'	ເX	ē
ແXະ	ae'	ແX	āe
ໂXະ	o'	ໂX	ō
ເXາະ	q'	X◌	ǭ
ເX	ue'	ເ◌ืX	ūe
ເXຍ	ia'	ເXຍ	īa
ເX◌ື ອ	eua'	ເX◌ື ອ	ēua
X◌ົ ວະ	oua'	XວX	ōua

The best way to learn how to pronounce these vowels is to sit down with a Lao person and practice them. Look carefully at the position of your Lao friend's mouth as you listen to him or her pronounce the vowels and try to imitate it as much as possible. Also, we will take a special look at some of the more difficult vowels below.

2.1.2 Special Vowels

T 18

ໄX	ai
ໃX	ai

ເຂົາ   ao
ຂໍາ   am

All of the special vowels are short, but unlike the standard vowels, they do not end with an abrupt glottal stop. The initial sound of all of the special vowels is "a", which joins with a second vowel sound. Because they are short vowels, the initial "a" sound must be pronounced as short as possible before gliding into the following sound, which can be dragged out a little longer.

The vowels ໄX and ໃX have the same sound ("ai"). In some dialects of Lao, particularly the Luang Prabang dialect, the ໃX is pronounced differently. There are a few words that have different meanings when spelled with one or the other, but they are still pronounced the same in the standard Vientiane dialect.

You will notice that the vowel ຂໍາ ("am") actually has a consonant ending. This is actually the vowel Xະ and the final consonant ມ. In old Lao this was written as ຂໍມ in some words[1], which makes sense once you understand the form changes for vowels with final consonants. However, ຂໍາ is still called a "special vowel" because of the unique form.

The vowels ໄX and ເຂົາ also have long counterparts which appear in the mixed vowels (ຂາຍ and ຂາວ, respectively). (The long counterpart of ຂໍາ is ຂາມ – "ām".)

2.2 Final Forms

Ten vowels in Lao change their form when a final consonant is added. It is important for you to know all of these to be able to correctly read and pronounce Lao words. We have already seen these changes previously in the mixed vowel chart. They are given to you here so that you can take special note of them.

---

[1] Present day Lao language is a mixture of Pali, Sanskrit and authentic Lao. In old Lao, the ຂໍາ was used for authentic Lao words and ຂໍມ was used on words that came from Pali-Sanskrit. The pronunciation is the same, but this allowed the reader to see the origin of the word. Recent revisions of the Lao language have unified the orthography and ຂໍມ, along with ຣ and a number of other items were dropped out.

Shapes and Sounds

xະ	⇒	x̆x	ດະ	⇒	ດັນ
ເxະ	⇒	ເx̆x	ເດະ	⇒	ເດັນ
ແxະ	⇒	ແx̆x	ແດະ	⇒	ແດັນ
ໂxະ	⇒	x̂x	ໂດະ	⇒	ດົນ
ເxາະ	⇒	x̆ອx	ເດາະ	⇒	ດັອນ
x̊	⇒	xອx	ດຳ	⇒	ດອນ
ເxຍ	⇒	x̆ຽx	ເດຍ	⇒	ດັຽນ
ເxຍ	⇒	xຽx	ເດຍ	⇒	ດຽນ
x̂ວະ	⇒	x̆ວx	ດົວະ	⇒	ດັວນ
x̂ວ	⇒	xວx	ດົວ	⇒	ດວນ

2.3 Mixed Vowels

Mixed vowels occur when either one of the two final "semi-vowel" consonants (ຍ and ວ) are added on to any of the standard vowels. Below is a chart that shows all of the possibilities. In the left hand column are all the standard vowels, short followed by long. (The form of the vowel shown in parentheses represents a form change when a final consonant is added to that particular vowel.) In the two right hand columns are the mixed vowels—one column for ຍ and the other column for ວ. You will notice there are many blank places in these columns with only a dash. These blank places represent mixtures that are not possible. You will also notice that many of the mixed vowels are in italics. Italics indicate that, though this particular mixed vowel is possible, it is rarely used in Lao, if ever. It is not important that you memorize the mixed vowels in italics.

The middle two columns show what other final consonants (one stop, one nasal) look like when they are added to the vowels. (The final stop ກ can be replaced with the final stops ດ and ບ. Similarly, the final nasal ງ can be replaced with the final nasals ນ and ມ.)

20

T 19

Lao Vowel (final cons. Form)	Final Stop ກ (k)	Final Nasal ງ (ng)	Final "Semi Vowel" ຍ (i)	Final "Semi Vowel" ວ (o/u)
xະ (xັx) / a' /	xັກ	xັງ	ໄx (xັຍ)	ເxົາ
xາ / ā /	xາກ	xາງ	xາຍ	xາວ
xິ / i' /	xິກ	xິງ	-	xິວ
xີ / ī /	xີກ	xີງ	-	xີວ
xຶ / eu' /	xຶກ	xຶງ	xືຍ	xຶວ
xື / ēu /	xືກ	xືງ	xືຍ	xືວ
xຸ / ou' /	xຸກ	xຸງ	xຸຍ	-
xູ / ōu /	xູກ	xູງ	xູຍ	-
ເxະ (ເxັx) / e' /	ເxັກ	ເxັງ	-	ເxັວ
ເx / ē /	ເxກ	ເxງ	ເxຍ	ເxວ
ແxະ (ແxັx) / ae' /	ແxັກ	ແxັງ	-	ແxັວ
ແx / āe /	ແxກ	ແxງ	-	ແxວ
ໂxະ (xັx) / o' /	xັກ	xັງ	ໂxຍ	ໂxວ
ໂx / o /	ໂxກ	ໂxງ	ໂxຍ	ໂxວ
ເxາະ (xັອx) / ǫ' /	xັອກ	xັອງ	xັອຍ	-
xໍ (xອx) / ǭ /	xອກ	xອງ	xອຍ	-
ເxິ / ue' /	ເxິກ	ເxິງ	ເxິຍ	ເxິວ
ເxີ / ūe /	ເxີກ	ເxີງ	ເxີຍ	ເxີວ
ເxຍ (xຽx) / ia' /	xຽກ	xຽງ	-	xຽວ
ເxຍ (xຽx) / īa /	xຽກ	xຽງ	-	xຽວ
ເxຶອ / eua' /	ເxຶອກ	ເxຶອງ	ເxຶອຍ	-
ເxືອ / ēua /	ເxືອກ	ເxືອງ	ເxືອຍ	-
xົວະ (xັວx) / oua' /	xັວກ	xັວງ	xັວຍ	-
xົວ (xວx) / ōua /	xວກ	xວງ	xວຍ	-

Shapes and Sounds

For the twelve mixed vowels that are commonly spoken, the ຢ is like adding an "i" sound to the existing vowel, and the ວ is like adding an "o" or "u" sound to the existing vowel.

T 20

×ๅຢ =	ā + i	=	āi (like "sigh")
×ๅວ =	ā + o	=	āo (like "now")
×ົວ =	i + u	=	iu (like "few")
×ຸຢ =	ou + i	=	oui (like "wee" but more rounded)
ເ×ວ =	ē + o	=	ēo (like "pay-oh")
ແ×ວ =	āe + o	=	āeo (similar to "shall")
ໂ×ຢ =	ō + i	=	ōi (like "boy")
×ອຢ =	ǫ + i	=	ǫi (similar to ōi, but with more of the "ǫ" sound as in "cost")
ເ×ືຢ =	ūe + i	=	ūei (like "ūe-i")
×ໂວ =	īa + o	=	īao (like "ī-ao")
ເ×ືອຢ =	ēua + i	=	ēuai (like "ēu-ai")
×ວຢ =	ōua + i	=	ōuai (like "ōu-ai")

The sounds of the last five mixed consonants above are difficult to represent with transliteration. It is important to spend time with a Lao person to get the correct pronunciation, or listen to a recording of the sound. It makes a big difference if you are able to master the sounds of the standard vowels before attempting the mixed vowels. Once you are able to pronounce the standard vowels the concept of adding another vowel sound to the end is more comprehensible.

Like the special vowels, mixed vowels cannot take a final consonant. (Technically, they already have one with the final "semi-vowels" ຢ and ວ.)

2.4 Pronunciation Tricks

2.4.1 Short and Long Vowels

English speakers often find it difficult to make the distinction between short and long vowels in Lao words. The most common error is to pronounce the short vowels too long. And, especially for words that end with a final consonant, it is also a common mistake to shorten the long vowels. (Examples of short and long vowel comparisons can be found in Track 21 of the accompanying audio. **T 21**)

For short vowels, the vowel sound is barely pronounced before beginning the sound of the final consonant or stop. The most important thing is to get your mouth in the right position for pronouncing the vowel and then pronounce the vowel as short as possible. That is the "trick" for pronouncing short vowels: pronounce them as short as possible. Practice these words below:

T 22

ຄະ   ຄັນ   ຄັງ
ໂຄະ   ຄິນ   ຄິງ
ຈິ   ຈິງ   ຈິບ
ຊຸ   ຊຸນ   ຊຸດ

For long vowels, the vowel sound is pronounced just a little longer than what might feel natural for a native English speaker. A "trick" that may help you to pronounce the long vowels is to extend the vowel sound as if it were two syllables. For example, let's use the Lao word ມາ (mā), "come". Try pronouncing it like "mah-ah" with two syllables, but instead of stopping in the middle sort of glide it together. This should give you about the right "length" of the vowel. Then smooth it out until it is one syllable, not two. For long vowels there can never be a final glottal stop. Try practicing this technique to correctly pronounce the following words with long vowels:

T 23

ຄາ   ຄານ   ຄາງ
ໂຄ   ໂຄນ   ໂຄງ

Shapes and Sounds

ຈື   ຈຶງ   ຈຶບ

ຊູ   ຊູມ   ຊູດ

2.4.2 Difficult Vowels

Vowels ຶX, Xຸ, and ເXຶ : This group of vowels, especially ຶX and ເXຶ, may be the most difficult Lao vowels for native English speakers to pronounce. They could all be transliterated with a "u" in English. However, none of them exactly exist in common English except for, perhaps, Xຸ. Here are some descriptions on how to pronounce these vowels:

ຶX   This vowel is similar to (but differant from) the "ew" in the word "chew" except that it is pronounced further back in the mouth and unrounded. (Actually it is more like the expression "eew" as in, "Eew! That's gross!"—pronounced toward the back of the mouth instead of the front.) "Unrounded" refers to the shape of your mouth during pronunciation. Lao people often pull back the corners of their mouths to pronounce this vowel, or to emphasize its correct pronunciation. However, instead of relying on this description have a the Lao speaker pronounce ຶX for you or listen to the examples given in the audio.

Xຸ   Of the three, this is probably the easiest to pronounce. It is similar to the "oo" in the word "boo". This vowel is rounded, so you want to make sure your lips form a round shape when pronouncing it correctly. It is also pronounced more toward the front of the mouth than "ou" typically is in English.

ເXຶ   This vowel is pronounced similarly to the "oo" in the English word "good" or like the "ou" in the word "could". However, it tends to come from a little deeper in the mouth. Perhaps a closer representation would be the "u" in the word "lurk" when pronounced in the British accent. (You certainly don't want to pronounce a hard "r" for this vowel.)

Shapes and Sounds

Following is a set of syllables you can use to practice these sounds:

T 24

ຄີ   ຄູ   ເຄີ
ຂີ   ຂູ   ເຂີ
ປີ   ປູ   ເປີ
ບີ   ບູ   ເບີ
ລີ   ລູ   ເລີ
ຊີ   ຊູ   ເຊີ

Vowels ເX and ແX : These vowels are present in the English language and do not present a pronunciation difficulty as much as a distinction difficulty. In general, ເX is pronounced as the "a" in the English word "made," and ແX is pronounced like the "a" in the English word "cat" (American English). However, at times the vowel ແX is pronounced in between the "a" in "cat" and the "e" in "pet", but still closer to the "a" in "cat".

The sound of ເX also appears to change somewhat when shortened and followed by a final stop. In that case (ເX̆X) sounds more like "e" in "pet" than it does "a" in "made". Below is a set of syllables you can use to practice these sounds:

T 25

ເຄ   ແຄ   ເຄັດ   ແຄັດ
ເຂ   ແຂ   ເຂັບ   ແຂັບ
ເປ   ແປ   ເປັາ   ແປັາ
ເບ   ແບ   ເບັດ   ແບັດ
ເລ   ແລ   ເລັບ   ແລັບ
ເຊ   ແຊ   ເຊັາ   ແຊັາ

Shapes and Sounds

Vowels ເX and X̊ : These two vowels should also not be too difficult for native English speaker to pronounce. The vowel ເX is pronounced like the "o" in the English word "go". The vowel X̊ is a little more difficult. It is pronounced similar the "o" in the word "cost" or the "aw" in the word "saw". However, the Lao X̊ is a little more rounded. As a result, it is sometimes confused with the vowel ເX by English speakers. One of the most common occasions this mistake arises is in the Lao phrase for "you're welcome" or "never mind": ບໍເປັນຫຍັງ (bọ bpen nyang). Many English speakers mistakenly say "bō bpen nyang". Below is a set of syllables you can use to practice these sounds:

T 26

ເດ   ດໍ
ເຊ   ຊໍ
ເຖ   ຖໍ
ເບ   ບໍ
ເລ   ລໍ
ເຣ   ຣໍ

(Examples of the vowels ເXຍ, ເX̃ອ, and X̃ວ, can also be found in the accompanying audio. **T 27**)

2.4.3 The "a" Sound

In English the letter "a" is typically associated with the sound of "a" in the word "made", or with the sound of "a" in the word "cat". It is also associated with the sound of "a" in the word "father". This latter pronunciation ("f<u>a</u>ther") is the sound of Xາ or Xະ in Lao. However, it is also common in English for the pronunciation of the letter "a" to shift to the "uh" sound, as in the words: "<u>a</u>bout", "<u>A</u>merica", or "<u>a</u>stounding".

Consequently, a common mistake native English speakers make is to pronounce the Xາ and Xະ in Lao with the "uh" (as in "butter") sound. Mostly, it is a matter of getting a little lazy with pronunciation, but be careful that you don't make this mistake. These vowels should be pronounced as the "a" in "father" (like the Spanish "a" is always pronounced).

2.4.4 The "i" Sound

The Lao language does not possess the "i" as in "sick" vowel which is common in English. But it is a common mistake for English speakers to make when they pronounce Lao words like ສິບ "sip" (ten). This word is pronounced like the word "seep" in English and is not pronounced like the word "sip" in English (as in, "May I have a sip of your drink?").

The X̊ and X̆ vowels in Lao should never be pronounced like the "i" in "sit" but always like the "ea" in "seat" (like the Spanish "i" is aways pronounced).

2.5 Recognition Tricks

One of the most difficult aspects of Lao vowels is that many of them have multiple "pieces". It is also difficult for native English speakers because vowels are written before, after, above, under or around the consonant they are pronounced with.

A "trick" to recognize a short vowel is the following:
- Any vowel with a X̆ (mai gkan) will be short.
- Any vowel with a X that does not have the tail (like the tails you see in X̊ or X̆) will be short.
- Any vowel with a Xະ will be short (and also not have a final consonant).
- Any vowel with X̥ will be short (rather than X̥, which is long).
- The special vowels ເX, ແX, ເXາ, and Xອ, are all short (and cannot have final consonants).

All short vowels will have one of these characteristics, and long vowels will not have any of these characteristics.

Take note of the short vowel ເXາະ (o'). Its appearance is very different from its long counterpart X (ọ). Also, when followed by a final consonant it will change to XອX (short) or XອX (long).

Shapes and Sounds

2.6 Flash Cards

As with the consonants, it is not necessary to know the correct order of the vowels. It is more important to be able to recognize them on sight and pronounce them correctly. A good way to practice Lao vowels is to make flash cards, each with one standard, special or mixed vowel on the front, and the transliteration on the back. Spend some time trying to memorize them, taking special note of long and short vowels, and then test yourself. Mix the order up and try again. After you have done this several times, remove the easiest ones from the stack and start over. If you find you are always confusing a few vowels, pull them out and take special note of the differences in the way it is written. If you do this well, within a few days you will have all the Lao vowels memorized and be able to recognize each one when you see it.

2.7 Writing Practice

As with consonants, most of the symbols used to write Lao vowels have a "head"—a little circle. To write the symbol you begin at the head. For the vowels X and X, begin at the left.

Native speakers and writers will write the letters less "perfect" than the printed version. First, learn to write the vowels according to the idealized form. Later, look at the more "relaxed" version of writing the vowels and become comfortable in your own style.

Practice writing the vowels by tracing them below. Remember to begin at the "head":

ຂະ	ຂາ	ຂະ	ຂາ
ຂ໌	ຂ໌	ຂ໌	ຂ໌
ຂ໌	ຂ໌	ຂ໌	ຂ໌
ຂຸ	ຂູ	ຂຸ	ຂູ
ເຂະ	ເຂ	ເຂະ	ເຂ
ແຂະ	ແຂ	ແຂະ	ແຂ
ໂຂະ	ໂຂ	ໂຂະ	ໂຂ

Shapes and Sounds

ເxາະ	×̊	ເxາະ	×̊
ເx̂	ເx̂	ເx̂	ເx̂
ເx̆ຍ	ເxຍ	ເx̆ຍ	ເxຍ
ເx̂ອ	ເx̂ອ	ເx̂ອ	ເx̂ອ
x̆ວະ	x̂ວ	x̆ວະ	x̂ວ
ໄx	ໃx	ໄx	ໃx
ເx̂າ	xຳ	ເx̂າ	xຳ
xາຍ	xາວ	xາຍ	xາວ
x̂ວ	xຸຍ	x̂ວ	xຸຍ
ເxວ	ແxວ	ເxວ	ແxວ
ໂxຍ	xອຍ	ໂxຍ	xອຍ
ເx̂ຍ	xຽວ	ເx̂ຍ	xຽວ
ເx̂ອຍ	xວຍ	ເx̂ອຍ	xວຍ

Now, practice a more "relaxed" form of writing the Lao vowels:

Xະ	Xາ	Xະ	Xາ
X̆	X̆	X̆	X̆
X̂	X̂	X̂	X̂
Xຸ	Xຸ	Xຸ	Xຸ
ເXະ	ເX	ເXະ	ເX
ແXະ	ແX	ແXະ	ແX
ໂXະ	ໂX	ໂXະ	ໂX

2.8 Spelling

It is helpful to know the names of the pieces of vowels. For example, suppose you are speaking with a Lao person and they use a new word you have not heard before. If it is difficult for you to understand how they pronounced this new word, you can spell it out (or have them spell it for you) and then you will know exactly how it is pronounced. Of course, if you write it down on paper it is not necessary to know the names of all the different pieces of vowels. But if in your situation you do not have the aid of writing, knowing these names is helpful.

For any piece of a vowel that would be a vowel on its own (such as ເ, າ, or ະ) you just say its name as that vowel. The word "vowel" in Lao is ສະຫລະ (sa'la'), and to discuss "ເ", for example, you would say ສະຫລະເອ (sa'la' ē). (Remember that ອ is the silent consonant.) The word used for consonant (when spelling) is ຕົວ (dtōua) or ໂຕ (dtō).

So, to spell ສາວ (sāo—"girl"), for example, you would say:
ຕົວ ສ   (dtōua sǭ)
ສະຫລະ ອາ   (sa'la' ā)
ຕົວ ວ   (dtōua vǭ)

Even though the ວ here is actually part of a mixed vowel, you refer to it as if it was a consonant for the purpose of spelling.

To spell the word ເມຍ (mīa—"wife") you can say it one of two ways:
ສະຫລະ ເອ   (sa'la' ē)
ຕົວ ມ   (dtōua mǭ)
ຕົວ ຍ   (dtōua nyǭ)

Or, more commonly:
ຕົວ ມ   (dtōua mǭ)
ສະຫລະ ເອຍ   (sa'la' īa)

For the special vowels you say the following:
ໄx   ສະຫລະໄອ ໄມ້ ມາຍ (sa'la' ai mai māi)
ໃx   ສະຫລະໃອ ໄມ້ ມ້ວນ (sa'la' ai mai mouan)
ເx̂າ   ສະຫລະ ເອົາ   (sa'la' ao)
xຳ   ສະຫລະ ອຳ   (sa'la' am)

2.9 Mai Gkan and Mai Gkong

Two marks that are not vowels on their own are x̌ and x̂. They are called ໄມ້ ກັນ (mai gkan) and ໄມ້ ກົງ (mai gkong) respectively. So, to spell a word like ຕົກລົງ (dtok long—"agree") you would say the following:

ຕົວ	ຕຳ	(dtōua dtǭ)
ໄມ້	ກົງ	(mai gkong)
ຕົວ	ກຳ	(dtōua gkǭ)
ຕົວ	ລຳ	(dtōua lǭ)
ໄມ້	ກົງ	(mai gkong)
ຕົວ	ງຳ	(dtōua ngǭ)

NOTES

3

TONES

3.1 The Importance of Tones

An argument can be made that tones are the most important aspect of the pronunciation of the Lao language. Many times when a foreigner mispronounces the tone of a Lao word, but pronounces everything else correctly, the Lao listener doesn't have any idea what he is talking about. It seems strange to the foreigner that the Lao person doesn't just run the sound of that word through all the tones to figure out what he might be saying. The Lao person thinks it strange that we would ever think those words sound remotely similar. This shows us that tones create an important distinction between words in Lao. While we may think ຫມາ (mā—rising tone—"dog") and ມ້າ (mā—falling tone—"horse") sound similar because they differ by only tone in pronunciation, the native Lao speaker hears them as differently as we hear "dog" and "horse" in English—words we would never confuse. In fact, if a native Lao speaker misunderstands what another person is saying, he is more likely to guess a different word with the same tone than the same word with a different tone.

An argument can also be made that tones aren't very important. Some tones have many variations. Also, when you talk about different dialects of Lao, the most prominent difference between Lao dialects is the tones. Each province and region of Laos has their own way of pronouncing the tones, and in some cases it is very different from the "standard" Vientiane dialect. Even around Vientiane different villages and areas have their own special variants to some of the tones. Yet, when these people talk with each other they are able to communicate just fine. They will certainly notice the "accent" of the other person, but it doesn't become a significant language barrier.

Similarly, many expatriates who come to Laos never learn to pronounce the tones properly and still manage to get along well with limited tonal proficiency. This is because the vast majority of words can be determined through context, if not correct pronunciation. They will often say words that the Lao listener doesn't understand and promptly adjust the tone to better communicate. In this situation just the knowledge that tones exist is helpful for communication.

All of these things considered, the better you are able to pronounce the tones the better off you will be. If your aim is not mere communication but proficiency in the Lao language then learning the tones is important. Lao people will even get excited and be amazed when they hear you speaking correctly and they will shower you with compliments. They will say that your sound is "fun". Usually that is enough motivation for the foreigner to continue to learn and practice the tones.

At the same time, don't let the tones discourage you. Realize that Lao people will be able to understand most of what you say even if you struggle with the tones. Tones are the most difficult aspect of the Lao language for native English speakers. As you attempt to hear and produce the tones there will be times when you swear that two sounds are identical that are supposed to be two different tones. You may feel like you are tone deaf and that you are not making any progress. Don't lose heart! You cannot learn the tones overnight, but the more exposure you have the more you will progress without even realizing it. You can do it!

3.2 The Six Basic Tones

There is no shortage of disagreement about Lao tones, how many there are and what they are like. Various people have offered descriptions of the Lao tones at different times, each description a little different. Some of the differences can be accounted for by varying dialects. Also, like all languages, Lao is continually changing. In recent times the National University of Laos settled upon one description for the "standard" Vientiane dialect.

Lao has six basic tones and two "special tones" tones. The basic tones are more universally accepted, but there is more disagreement about the other two tones, which we will look at in the next section. For convenience, the tones have been numbered as in the diagram below.

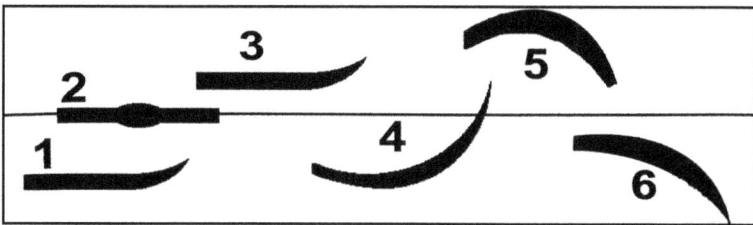

Description of Lao Tones	
Tone 1	Low level tone (slight rising at the end)
Tone 2	Mid level tone
Tone 3	High level tone (slight rising at the end)
Tone 4	Low rising tone
Tone 5	High falling tone (short rise before the fall)
Tone 6	Mid falling tone

This description is adapted from the description offered by the National University of Laos. In particular, this diagram shows the "fades" and "cut-offs" of the tonal contours.

Tones 1 and 3, you will notice, have the same shape. Both of them fade and rise slightly at the end. Tone 1 is pronounced at the low end of the normal speaking range and Tone 3 at the high end of the normal speaking range. Tone 1 will "feel" low to the native English speaker, but don't try to go very low. Tone 3 may "feel" a little high, but not very high. To some, Tone 3 won't feel high at all. Don't make the mistake of pronouncing 3 with a falsetto pitch. The fade and rise of Tones 1 and 3 sound very natural. Words said with these tones sound similar to how we would pronounce a "free standing" word in English (but not like we would pronounce it at the end of a sentence or as an answer to a question).

Because Tones 1 and 3 occur in situations that never distinguish meaning and because their contour is the same, many linguists combine these tones and describe the Lao language as having five basic tones. That is fine if you prefer to think of it that way and you can proceed to pronounce all of the words with Tone 1 and Tone 3 with the exact same tone (such as Tone 3 is described). However, words that fit the category of Tone 1 will often have many tone variations, whereas words that fit the category of Tone 3 will not. Consequently, in this book we keep them separate, in line with the National University's description, to better understand the tonal dynamics.

Tone 2 is pronounced in the mid-range of the voice. Many native English speakers have a difficult time distinguishing Tone 2 from Tone 3 as the "pitch" level is not too different. However, Tone 2 does not end with a fade and rise. Instead it stops level or slightly down. This is the distinguishing characteristic of Tone 2. The "bump" in the middle of Tone 2 in the diagram above may prove helpful for you to hear and pronounce Tone 2. To some, the volume or intensity of Tone 2 appears to increase in the middle pronunciation. In actuality, it is a very slight rise and fall of the tone accompanied by a volume that does not fade (as the volume fades at the end of Tones 1 and 3).

Tone 4 may be the easiest of all of the tones for the native English speaker to produce since there are no others very similar to it. Tone 4 is a rising tone that begins low and actually dips before rising and fading. It is not the same tone as the rise at the end of a question in English. Instead, since it begins low it will "feel" low when you begin to pronounce it.

Tone 5 may be the easiest of the tones to "hear" when you are listening to a Lao person speak. It starts high and rises a little before falling fast. The character of Tone 5 could be compared to the sound a child makes when he is trying to take his toy away from another child and whines "It's mine!"

Tone 6 is similar to Tone 5 but lower. It starts in the low mid range and falls. However, unlike Tone 5, it does not rise as much before it falls.

Tones 5 and 6 can occur on words that do not have final stops and on words that do. When there are no final stops the sound tends to fade more. But in the case when there are final stops, the sound tends to stop abruptly without the fade. In the diagram above you see the more abrupt stop indicated on Tone 5 and the fade on Tone 6.

Pronouncing the following series of words can produce the six tones:

T 28

ກາ (1)   ຄ່າ (2)   ຄາ (3)   ຂາ (4)   ຄ້າ (5)   ຂ້າ (6)
crow   value   syllable   leg   to trade   to kill

Below is a real graph of a Lao speaker pronouncing the six words above. You can see the shapes of the six tones very well here, from left to right Tones 1-6. This particular speaker pronounces a variant form of Tone 1 that is similar to Tone 6. Other Lao speakers would pronounce Tone 1 such that the shape of it would be identical to the contour for Tone 3 that you see below, but in the low range.

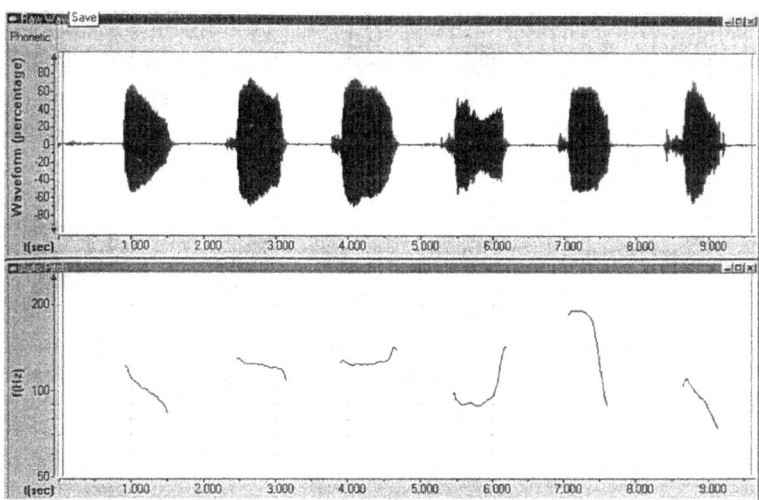

The top portion of the graph shows the volume intensity of the word while it was spoken. Each one corresponds to the tone contour immediately below it. Notice the contour for Tone 2 and how it falls slightly at the end, and how Tone 3 rises slightly at the end.

3.3 Tones 7 and 8

There are two more tones that occur only with short vowels with final stops. They are Tones 7 and 8. Previously, words that fell into this category (short vowel with a final stop) were listed as Tones 3 and 2. Because they occur only in specific circumstances, many linguists wish to simplify things by describing them as existing rather than separate tones. However, for the purposes of language learning it isn't always advantageous to simplify and by separating Tones 7 and 8 from the basic six, Lao language learners can gain some good insight on how to correctly pronounce words that fall into these categories.

That said, there is still some disagreement on what these two tones should be. Some people pronounce Tone 7 higher that Tone 8, and others do the reverse. It can be confusing for the person who is trying to learn these tones as there are a good number of words that vary only by this tone difference. (Listen to Track 60 in the accompanying audio file.)

The essential difference between Tones 7 and 8 is that one is a rising tone and the other a falling tone. The reason they are usually not described as such is because they are on words that have a short vowel and a final stop and are pronounced very quickly as a result. The "rising" and the "falling" of these tones isn't apparent as on longer words. Below is a diagram of all eight tones in Lao, which includes Tones 7 and 8.

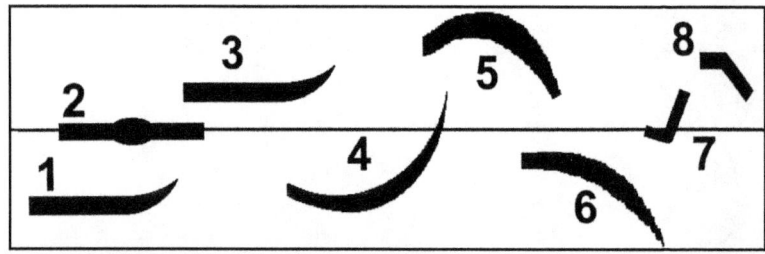

	Description of Lao Tones
Tone 1	Low level tone (slight rising at the end)
Tone 2	Mid level tone
Tone 3	High level tone (slight rising at the end)

Tone 4	Low rising tone
Tone 5	High falling tone (short rise before the fall)
Tone 6	Mid falling tone
Tone 7	Short mid rising tone (actually falls a little then rises)
Tone 8	Short high falling tone

The following words are examples of words with Tones 7 and 8.

T 29

ກັດ(7)   ັດ(8)   ຂັດ(7)
to bite   to copy   syllable

Below is a real graph of a Lao speaker pronouncing the three words above. You can see the shapes of Tones 7 and 8 very well here. From left to right it is Tone 7, Tone 8, Tone 7.

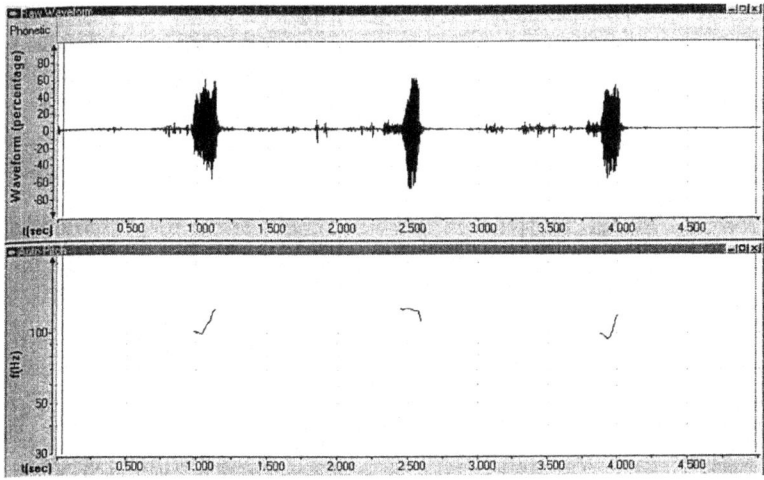

Notice that Tone 8 (in the middle) is slightly higher than Tone 7 for this speaker. Actually, according to this speaker, Tone 8 starts higher than Tone 7 starts, but ends lower than Tone 7 ends.

The best way to learn Tones 7 and 8, as with all of the tones, is to listen to a native speaker pronounce them and repeat them and repeat them as closely as possible. Some Lao speakers pronounce

Tone 8 lower than Tone 7, but even when this occurs the Tone 8 still falls a little and the Tone 7 rises. Consequently, the rising and falling of these two tones is the essential difference. It may seem very difficult to hear at first, but with a lot of practice you will be able to successfully distinguish and pronounce these two tones.

3.4 Special Tone Mai Tī

There is one other tone that is occasionally encountered. This tone is produced when the tone mark ໄມ້ຕີ (mai tī): Ẍ is placed on a word. (Tone marks and spelling will be addressed in Chapter Five.) This tone is not found in common Lao but is used almost exclusively for onomatopoeia (words that mimic the sound of something, like "bang!"). We can call this Tone 9 even though it is usually not numbered or listed. Tone 9 is a high and quick rising tone. In the row of words below you will see the word ແປນ (bpāen) with all of the possible tone marks on them. Mai tī is second from the right. Below the row of words are the graphs from these words when pronounced by a Lao speaker.

T 30

ແປນ(1)　　ແປ່ນ(2)　　ແປ້ນ(5)　　ແປັນ(9)　　ແປ໋ນ(4)

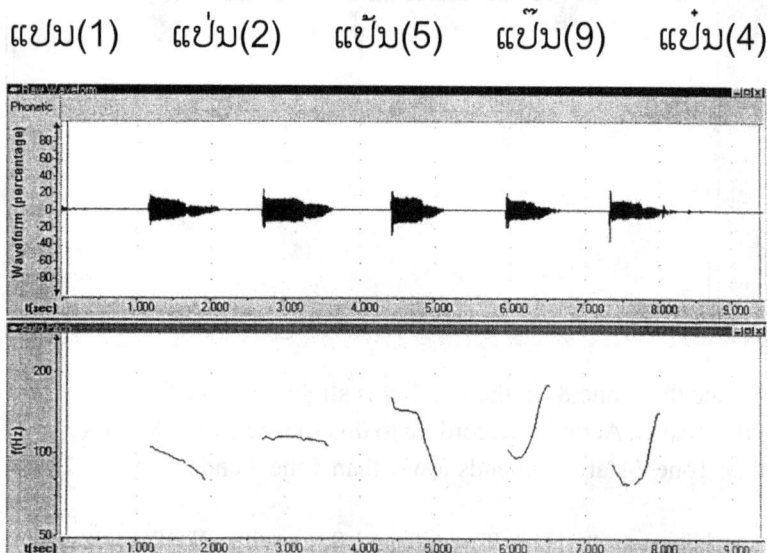

You can easily see Tone 9 (second from the right) being higher than Tone 4, and pronounced shorter (more quickly). Though Tone 9

exists in Lao, it is rare. Consequently, it is not very important to know this one.

3.5 Pronouncing Tones on Short Vowels (without a final stop)

The important thing to remember when pronouncing short vowels is to pronounce the vowel sound as short as possible. Lengthening the vowel sound at all will make it sound like a long vowel and will thus change the meaning of the word. Some native English speakers might find this especially difficult when pronouncing the special vowels.

An example may be found when comparing the words ກາຍ (pass) and ໄກ (far). The only difference between these two words is the length of the vowel. Since this vowel is a glide, it mixes the vowel "a" and "i". The word with the long vowel can be written as "gkāi," and the short "gkai". The trick for pronouncing the difference is to lengthen the "a" on the first word, ກາຍ, and to keep it short on the second word, ໄກ. It is necessary to keep the "a" part of the sound short for ໄກ, but if you lengthen the "i" part of the vowel it won't change its meaning. Consequently, you can pronounce it like "gkaī".

This same "trick" is true for the special vowel ເXາ. The word ສາວ (girl) and ເສົາ (column) differ only by vowel length. As the example before, ສາວ should be pronounced with the long "a"— "sāo". On the other hand, ເສົາ can be pronounced as "sao" or "saō" with the "a" part of the vowel being short.

A common mistake when pronouncing the various tones on words with the special vowels is to lengthen the vowel in order to achieve the correct tone contour. Be careful not to make this mistake. Instead, think about the tone contour being pronounced mostly on the second part of the special vowel (the "i" for ເX or ໄX, and the "o" for ເXາ), which can be stretched out a little more to achieve the correct tone.

The same is true for short vowels with final nasals. Because the final sounds in these words are consonants and not vowels it is a very common mistake to lengthen the vowel sound in order to pronounce the various tones. However, with these words—short vowels with final nasals—the tone is pronounced mostly on the final nasal consonant. So a word like ຫັງ (skin) is pronounced with the rising tone being heard mostly on the final ງ ("ng"), while the "a" vowel is still pronounced as short as possible.

Shapes and Sounds

Practice pronouncing the various tones on these real Lao words and syllables below. Remember to keep the initial vowel sound as short as possible for the special vowels, and to keep the vowel sound as short as possible on the words with final nasals.

T 31

ໄກ(1)   ໄກ່(2)   ໃກ້(5)
far   chicken   near

ເຊົາ(3)   ເຊົ່າ(2)   ເຊົ້າ(5)   ເສົາ(4)   ເສົ້າ(6)
to stop   to rent   morning   column   sad

ບງ(3)   ບົ່ງ(2)   ບົ້ງ(5)   ຫນັງ(4)   ຫນັ້ງ(6)
syllable   to sit   syllable   skin   syllable

ຄັນ(3)   ຄັ່ນ(2)   ຄັ້ນ(5)   ຂັນ(4)   ຂັ້ນ(6)
to scratch   to score cloth   to knead   to crow   step

3.6 Tones on Final Particles

A special category of words in Lao is final particles. These words can be one of the most difficult aspects of the Lao language for native English speakers who are studying Lao. That is because they don't carry a particular assigned meaning but are used to emphasize or soften a statement or command. Final particles, which especially abound in spoken Lao, are often pronounced with a different tone than what is written. And sometimes altering the tone on a final particle can give it a different shade of meaning in a particular context. But even with these variances, they are always written the same when in the final particle position and usually do not carry a tone mark, even though some of them are pronounced as if they do.

Below is a list of final particles in common Lao sentences. The last word in each sentence is the final particle and is underlined. The first column of numbers is the number of the tone according to how the word is spelled, and the second number is the actual spoken tone.

T 32

Sentence	Written Tone #	Actual Tone
ເຊີນກິນເລີຍ! Please eat!	3	3
ເຈົ້າຢາກໄດ້ກໍາເອົາສາ! You would like this; go ahead and take it!	4	4
ເຈົ້າຊິໄປຫລວງພະບາງບໍ? Are you going to go to Luang Prabang	1	4
ເຊີນລາວເຂົ້າມາແມ! Invite him in!	3	5
ລາວກໍເປັນຄົນດີຢູ່ນາ! He is a pretty good person!	3	5
ແມ່ນຄວາມລາວເວົ້າຕິ! It is as he says, (uncertain)?	1	5
ມ່ວນແທ້ນໍ! This is very fun!	3	5
ຂອບໃຈເດີ! Thank you!	1	5

You will notice that on the first two examples the tone isn't different. There is no rule for knowing when the tone shifts—you just have to memorize the exceptions when you learn the final particles. For now, it is just helpful to know these tone-shifts exist so you will understand what is happening when you encounter one.

Also, take special notice of the word ບໍ in the example that is a question. This word effectively means "no" and is the word that makes a statement a yes-or-no question when placed at the end of a sentence. When used in the middle of a sentence (meaning "no" or "not") it occurs with a tone mark as ບໍ່, and is pronounced with Tone 2 (mid-level tone). At the end of a sentence, however, the tone mark is dropped. And though it would normally be pronounced with Tone 1 (low-level tone) when written like this, in this situation it is pronounced with Tone 4 (low-rising tone).

3.7 Tone Variations

It is not practical or necessary to discuss all of the different tone variations that exist in Lao. Many of them are associated with different provinces or regions around the country. (For example, Tone 4—low rising tone—is pronounced high around Luang Prabang.)

The tone that probably has the most variations is Tone 1. That is because Tone 1 only occurs on middle class consonants (to be discussed in the next chapter) without final stops. Those consonant sounds cannot be achieved with any other consonants so the tone isn't important for distinguishing their meaning. Some variations of Tone 1 are:

1. Falling-Rising Tone (common in some parts of Vientiane)
2. Mid Falling Tone (like the speaker in the graphs)
3. High Level Tone with slight rising at the end (same as Tone 3)[1]

In some places Tone 6 is pronounced like Tone 5 and the different meanings of words are understood from context. However, it is not uncommon for people who pronounce Tone 6 like Tone 5 to adjust to the standard pronunciation when directly comparing words that differ only by those two tones.

All of the different dialects of Lao have not been studied and analyzed. Perhaps sometime in the future linguists will do

---

[1] It is interesting to note that these three variations could roughly compare to Tones 4, 6 and 3 respectively. If you put a mai ēk, x̀, on words that have Tone 1, they would become Tone 2. If you put a mai thō, x̃, on them, they would become Tone 5. Consequently, Tone 1 does not have variants that sound like Tone 2 or Tone 5, but rather that sound like Tones 3, 4 and 6.

Shapes and Sounds

a comprehensive study of tone variations throughout Laos. As it stands now, the Vientiane dialect is considered "standard Lao". It is what is written and taught in Lao schools, and what is most accepted in the government. Consequently, the Vientiane dialect is recommended as the dialect to learn for expatriates living in Laos. However, if one is going to be working in a particular part of the country it would be beneficial to become familiar with the particular tones in that area. Since the few materials that describe the Lao language deal almost exclusively with the Vientiane dialect, it is best to learn it first to have a basis for comparison should you ever learn a different one.

3.8 Tones in Sentences

When Lao words are spoken in isolation the tone takes on the "idealized" form. However, when speaking in full, normal sentences, the tones may be slightly different. More than anything, they are shortened to aid in fast speech. Native English speakers will find it especially difficult to try to keep up with all the different tones in a sentence when trying to speak quickly. Below is a sentence that was recorded in both an idealized and ordinary fashion. (It says, "I learn Lao language at Dong Dok.") The tone graph of both recordings follows below.

T 33-34

ຂ້ອຍ(6) ຮຽນ(3) ພາ(3) ສາ(4) ລາວ(3) ຢູ່(2) ດົງ(1) ໂດກ(6)

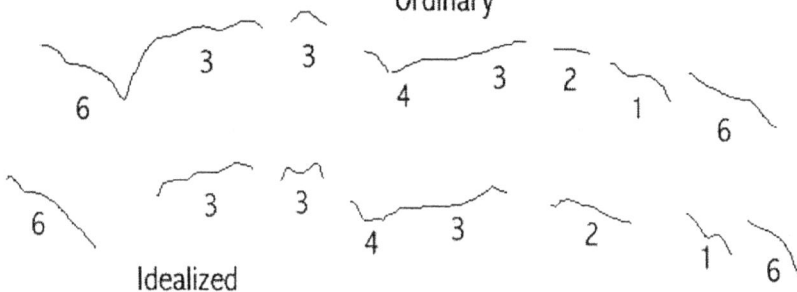

There is not a lot of difference in the shapes of the tones, except that they are shorter in length. Now, the "ordinary" version that was recorded was still spoken clearly. If the same sentence was spoken less clearly there would undoubtedly be some marked differences. But the similarity between the "idealized" and "ordinary" versions here further emphasizes the importance of tones in Lao. (Other examples of tones in Lao sentences, both idealized and ordinary, can be found in Tracks 35-42 of the accompanying audio. **T 35-42**)

NOTES

4

LEARNING THE TONES
WITHOUT KNOWING HOW TO READ AND WRITE LAO

There are many different methods for learning a second language. Many methods do not rely on an ability to read and write the target language. And with Lao, this is also recommended. It is a good idea to get a good conversational base before learning to read and write Lao. This will force you to rely on your listening ability to "hear" the tone of the word the Lao person is saying rather than simply deducing the correct tone after having him or her write it down. At the same time, learning the Lao orthography will be helpful at the appropriate time. When you do, you will discover things about the sounds and tones of Lao you never completely understood before.

Learning to distinguish and pronounce the tones of Lao is certainly possible without relying on the written language. This chapter will present a step by step procedure you can use, along with the help of an audio recorder or the accompanying audio for this text, and a Lao friend.

STEP 1: Take some time to become familiar with the tone descriptions of the eight Lao tones in Chapter 3. Simply knowing which tones exist will help you go a long way in your ability to hear and speak them. Don't worry about the tone rules from Chapter 5 concerning what combinations of consonants, vowels and tone marks determine which tone. Just familiarize yourself with the pitch and contour of the eight tones.

STEP 2: Make a list of simple Lao words that represent each of the Lao tones, or use the list below. As much as possible, find real words that differ only by the tone in pronunciation. Below is a sample list. (All of these words are real Lao words or syllables in words.)

Shapes and Sounds

T 43

1. gkao (1)	gkao (2)	khao (3)	khao (4)	gkao (5)	khao (6)
ເກົາ	ເກົ໋າ	ເຄົາ	ເຂົາ	ເກົ້າ	ເຂົ້າ
to scratch	old	syllable	horn	nine	rice

T 44

2. gkā (1)	khā (2)	khā (3)	khā (4)	khā (5)	khā (6)
ກາ	ຄ່າ	ຄາ	ຂາ	ຄ້າ	ຂ້າ
crow	value	syllable	leg	to trade	to kill

T 45

3. sao (2)	sao (3)	sao (4)	sao (5)	sao (6)
ເຊົ່າ	ເຊົາ	ເສົາ	ເຊົ້າ	ເສົ້າ
to rent	to stop	column	morning	sad

T 46

4. mai (2)	mai (4)	mai (5)	mai (6)
ໃໝ່	ໄໝ	ໄມ້	ໃໝ້
new	silk	wood	to burn

T 47

5. mā (2)	mā (3)	mā (4)	mā (5)
ໝ່າ	ມາ	ໝາ	ມ້າ
to soak	to come	dog	horse

Or, make a list of words that have no meaning but have syllables that vary only by tone. The list below is a good example. The first half of the list shows all the possibilities for the word with a short vowel and the second half shows all the possibilities for the word with a long vowel. (Therefore, you can also compare the short and long vowel sounds here, too.)

T 48

1. nang (3)	nang (2)	nang (5)
ນັງ	ນັ່ງ	ນັ້ງ

nang (4)	nang (2)	nang (6)
ຫັງ	ຫັງ	ຫັ້ງ
nāng (3)	nāng (2)	nāng (5)
ນາງ	ນ່າງ	ນ້າງ
nāng (4)	nāng (2)	nāng (6)
ຫາງ	ຫ່າງ	ຫັ້າງ

T 49

2. khat (8)   kha' (8)   khat (7)   kha' (7)   gkat (7)   gka' (7)
   ຄັດ   ຄະ   ຂັດ   ຂະ   ກັດ   ກະ

STEP 3: Record a Lao person speaking these words correctly onto a digital recorder, or use the accompanying audio file for this text.

STEP 4: Listen to your recording or the accompanying audio file over and over. Compare the sounds of the different tones. When you listen to a line of words, first listen to the entire word. Then, listen to how each word is pronounced initially. Next, listen to the pronunciation of the middle of each word. Finally, listen to the pronunciation of the end of each word. Note and compare any differences. It may take you hundreds of times before you are able to detect the essential differences between similar but different tones.

STEP 5: Listen to your recording or the audio file again, this time pronouncing the words in unison with the sound you hear. Try to produce the sound as identical to the recorded audio as possible.

STEP 6: Identify which tones you most often confuse. Make a list of word pairs that differ by those tones. A few examples of real Lao words might be:

T 50

1. nang (3)   nang (2)
   ນັງ   ນັ່ງ
   syllable   to sit

Shapes and Sounds

mā (3)
ມາ
to come

mā (2)
ໝ່າ
to soak rice

sao (3)
ເຊົາ
to stop

sao (2)
ເຊົ່າ
to rent

khā (3)
ຄາ
syllable

khā (2)
ຄ່າ
value

ching (1)
ຈິງ
true

ching (2)
ຈິ່ງ
syllable

gkīao (1)
ກຽວ
coil

gkīao (2)
ກ່ຽວ
concerning

T 51

2. sā (5)
    ຊ້າ
    slow

    sā (6)
    ສ້າ
    type of tree

    khā (5)
    ຄ້າ
    to trade

    khā (6)
    ຂ້າ
    to kill

    thao (5)
    ເທົ້າ
    lean against

    thao (6)
    ເຖົ້າ
    old

    sao (5)
    ເຊົ້າ
    morning

    sao (6)
    ເສົ້າ
    sad

khǭp (5) ຄອບ syllable	khǭp (6) ຂອບ edge
sāt (5) ຊາດ nation	sāt (6) ສາດ mat

T 52

3.

hak (8) ຮັກ to love	hak (7) ຫັກ to break
het (8) ເຮັດ to do, to make	het (7) ເຫັດ mushroom
vat (8) ວັດ temple	vat (7) ຫວັດ cold (sickness)
phak (8) ພັກ to rest	phak (7) ຜັກ vegetable
phit (8) ພິດ poison	phit (7) ຜິດ wrong
sout (8) ຊຸດ set	sout (7) ສຸດ end
mot (8) ມົດ ant	mot (7) ຫມົດ finished, all

STEP 7: Record these pairs onto your device or find them on the accompanying audio file. Listen to them as before. Continue to listen to them over and over until you can distinguish and produce the different sounds.

STEP 8: Practice tones with a Lao friend. Do the following two-part procedure:

1. Have your Lao friend pronounce words randomly chosen from your list without indicating which word they have chosen. Listen to the Lao person's pronunciation of the word and choose the word in the list you think they are saying. Continue to do this until you can successfully choose all the right words.
2. This time switch roles. Pronounce words from your list and have your Lao friend point to the word they heard you say. See if they choose the one you were attempting to say. Continue to do this until you can successfully pronounce all of the words.

Following these eight steps for learning to distinguish and pronounce the Lao tones is not easy work! It takes a lot of time and effort. But if you follow this program diligently you will be able to hear and speak Lao tones successfully. It is not as difficult as it seems in the beginning and once you begin to succeed you will know it was well worth the effort. Have fun!!!

NOTES

5
TONE RULES

There are four things in the Lao orthography (system of writing) that determine which tone a word will have. They are the class of the initial consonant, the presence of a final stop, tone marks and long or short vowels.

5.1 Consonant Classes

Lao consonants are divided into three classes. The classes are called high (ສູງ), middle (ກາງ) and low (ຕ່ຳ). The names of the classes of consonants should not be confused with the natural tone of the consonant. The names of the classes are misnomers: High class consonants have a low rising tone (Tone 4); low class consonants have a high tone (Tone 3); and mid class consonants have a low tone (Tone 1). Take care not to confuse the name of the class of consonants with the tone of the consonant.

Below are the consonants divided into their classes. HCC stands for "High Class Consonant". MCC for "Middle Class Consonant" and LCC for "Low Class Consonant".

HCC ຂ ສ ຖ ຜ ຝ ຫ (rising tone consonants)
MCC ກ ຈ ດ ຕ ບ ປ ຍ ອ (low tone consonants)
LCC ຄ ງ ຊ ຍ ທ ນ ມ ຟ ຣ ລ ວ ຮ (high tone consonants)

It is important to learn which class each of the consonants belongs to. Even if you are not able to list all of the consonants that belong to each class, it is important to be able to recognize their classification on sight.

When pronouncing the name of a consonant (done by adding the vowel ◌ໍ to the consonant), HCCs will have the rising Tone 4,

53

MCCs will have the low Tone 1, and LCCs will have the high Tone 3. It is good to practice the alphabet pronouncing all of the letters according to their tones and remembering them that way.

The sound of each of the MCCs is unique—there are no other consonants in the other classes that have the same consonant sound. However, as you have probably already seen, some of the LCCs have HCCs that match the sound but differ by tone. There are six of them:

LCC	HCC
ຄ	ຂ
ຊ	ສ
ທ	ຖ
ຜ	ຜ
ຟ	ຝ
ຮ	ຫ

The remaining six LCCs also have HCCs that mirror them when the consonant ຫ is added to the front of the LCC.

LCC	HCC
ງ	ຫງ
ຍ	ຫຍ
ນ	ຫນ or ໜ
ມ	ຫມ or ໝ
ລ	ຫລ or ຫຼ
ວ	ຫວ

So, together, the LCCs and HCCs produce 12 pairs:

LCC	HCC
ຄ	ຂ
ງ	ຫງ
ຊ	ສ
ຍ	ຫຍ
ທ	ຖ

Shapes and Sounds

ນ	ຫນ or ໜ
ມ	ໝ
ຍ	ໜ
ປ	ຫມ or ໝ
ລ	ຫລ or ຫຼ
ວ	ຫວ
ຣ	ຫ

The new HCC members that are written with the ຫ are pronounced with the rising Tone 4 rather than the high Tone 3.

You will also notice that there are three new symbols: ໜ, ໝ, and ຫຼ.
  These are interchangeable with ຫນ, ຫມ and ຫລ, respectively. Take some time practicing writing these symbols, especially noting the difference between ໜ and ໝ.

ໜ ໜ ໜ ໜ ໜ ໜ ໜ ໜ ໜ ໜ ໜ

ໝ ໝ ໝ ໝ ໝ ໝ ໝ ໝ ໝ ໝ ໝ

ຫຼ ຫຼ ຫຼ ຫຼ ຫຼ ຫຼ ຫຼ ຫຼ ຫຼ ຫຼ ຫຼ

ໜ ໜ ໜ ໜ ໜ ໜ ໜ ໜ ໜ ໜ ໜ

ໝ ໝ ໝ ໝ ໝ ໝ ໝ ໝ ໝ ໝ ໝ

ຫຼ ຫຼ ຫຼ ຫຼ ຫຼ ຫຼ ຫຼ ຫຼ ຫຼ ຫຼ ຫຼ

   Take a look at the chart below. This shows the three basic, or "natural" tones associated with each of the consonant classes. The X in the chart represents the initial consonant of a word. There are also a few examples of words for each tone.

Shapes and Sounds

NATURAL TONES	
CONSONANT CLASS	x + Long vowel with no final consonant, or Any vowel with a final nasal or semi-vowel consonant, or Special vowel
High Class Consonants	Tone 4 ✓ ຂາ ຂາງ ຂັງ ຂາຍ ໄຂ
Middle Class Consonants	Tone 1 — ກາ ກາງ ກັງ ກາຍ ໄກ
Low Class Consonants	Tone 3 ⁓ ຄາ ຄາງ ຄັງ ຄາຍ ໄຄ

5.2 Final Stops

There are four final stops in Lao. They are ກ, ດ, ບ, and the final glottal stop (unwritten) that occurs on short vowels with no final consonants.

Words with final stops cannot take tone marks in Lao. Consequently, words with final stops are limited to having Tones 5, 6, 7 or 8.

HCCs with long vowels and a final stop consonant will have Tone 6. HCCs with short vowels and a final stop (ກ, ດ, ບ, or glottal stop) will have Tone 7.

MCCs with long vowels and a final stop consonant will have Tone 6. MCCs with short vowels and a final stop (ກ, ດ, ບ, or glottal stop) will have Tone 7.

LCCs with long vowels and a final stop consonant will have Tone 5. LCCs with short vowels and a final stop (ກ, ດ, ບ, or glottal stop) will have Tone 8.

Take a look at the chart below. This shows the four tones produced when words end with final stops. The X in the chart represents the initial consonant of a word. There are also a few examples of words for each tone.

TONES ON WORDS WITH FINAL STOPS (can't have standard tone marks)		
CONSONANT CLASS	x + ກ, ດ, ບ, Long vowels with final stop consonant	x + Short vowel with no final consonant (glottal stop), or Short vowel with no final consonant
High Class Consonants	Tone 6 ˇ ຂາກ ຂາດ ຂາບ	Tone 7 ´ ຂະ ຂັກ ຂັດ ຂັບ
Middle Class Consonants	Tone 6 ˇ ກາກ ກາດ ກາບ	Tone 7 ´ ກະ ກັກ ກັດ ກັບ
Low Class Consonants	Tone 5 ˆ ຄາກ ຄາດ ຄາບ	Tone 8 ˋ ຄະ ຄັກ ຄັດ ຄັບ

5.3 Tone Marks

There are two standard tone marks in Lao and two special marks. The standard tone marks are ໄມ້ ເອກ (mai ēk): X́, and ໄມ້ ໂທ (mai thō): X̂. These are very common in Lao and it is important to know how they are used.

ໄມ້ ເອກ (mai ēk): X́ always produces Tone 2 on the word it is placed upon. It does not matter if the initial consonant is HCC, MCC or LCC—it will always be Tone 2. Consequently, ໄມ້ ເອກ is the easiest of all the tone marks to understand.

ໄມ້ ໂທ (mai thō): X̂ always makes the word it is placed on a falling tone—Tone 5 or 6. On MCCs and LCCs ໄມ້ ໂທ produces Tone 5. On HCCs ໄມ້ ໂທ produces Tone 6.

Take a look at the chart below. This shows the three tones produced when words appear with a standard tone mark. The X in the chart represents the initial consonant of a word. There are also a few examples of words for each tone. Notice that for X́ it is always Tone 2. Also, remember that these tone marks will not appear on words with final stops.

Shapes and Sounds

TONES ON WORDS WITH TONE MARKS		
CONSONANT CLASS	ຂ̇	ຂ̃
High Class Consonants	Tone 2 — ຂ່າ ຂ່າງ ຂັ້ງ ຂ່າຍ ໄຂ່	Tone 6 ⌣ ຂ້າ ຂ້າງ ຂັ້ງ ຂ້າຍ ໄຂ້
Middle Class Consonants	Tone 2 — ກ່າ ກ່າງ ກັ້ງ ກ່າຍ ໄກ່	Tone 5 ⌢ ກ້າ ກ້າງ ກັ້ງ ກ້າຍ ໄກ້
Low Class Consonants	Tone 2 — ຄ່າ ຄ່າງ ຄັ້ງ ຄ່າຍ ໄຄ່	Tone 5 ⌢ ຄ້າ ຄ້າງ ຄັ້ງ ຄ້າຍ ໄຄ້

The two special tone marks are ໄມ້ ຕີ (mai tī): X̃, and ໄມ້ ຈັດຕະວາ (mai chattavā): X̟. These two tone marks are rare and many Lao people are unsure of how to pronounce words that have them. They are used for onomatopoeia (words that mimic the sound of something, like "bang!") almost exclusively. Both X̃ and X̟ only appear on MCCs. However, unlike X̀ and X̃, X̃ and X̟ can both be placed on words that have final stops.

ໄມ້ ຕີ (mai tī) X̃, as discussed in the previous chapter, produces a high and quick rising tone. We have dubbed this Tone 9 for our purposes. It may also be used on other words for onomatopoeia to indicate a completely different sound than what would normal be produced.

ໄມ້ ຈັດຕະວາ (mai chattavā) X̟ produces a low rising tone, Tone 4, on MCCs. It may also be used on other words for onomatopoeia to indicate a completely different sound than what would normally be produced.

5.4 Tone Chart

The following chart encapsulates all the tone rules for standard Lao. The X in the chart represents the initial consonant. The left hand column indicates the three different consonant classes the initial consonant will fall into: HCC, MCC or LCC.

There are three categories of words that do not have any tone marks. The first category is words with long vowels and no final consonant, or, words with long or short vowels that have either a final nasal or final semi-vowel consonant (but not a final stop). The second category is words that have long vowels and end with a final stop consonant. The third category is words with a short vowel and a final stop (either a final stop consonant ກ, ດ and ບ, or a final glottal stop).

> *Remember, a final glottal stop is not written in Lao. Instead it occurs when words with short vowels do not have a final consonant. The sound stops abruptly without the aid of a final consonant. However, the final glottal stop plays the exact same role of a final stop consonant in determining the tone of the word.*

There are two categories of words that have tone marks—one for X̀ and another for X̂. It doesn't matter if these words have long or short vowels or whether or not they have final consonants (nasals or semi-vowel consonants). However, since the standard tone marks cannot appear on words with a final stop, these words will not have a final ກ, ດ and ບ, or a final glottal stop.

The numbers indicate the number of the tone as previously described in Chapter 3. Also, the tone contours are placed in each cell for you convenience.

Spend some time studying this chart until you have a clear understanding of how to use it. Then choose some random Lao words and use the chart to figure out which tones they should be pronounced with. You can double-check this with a Lao person to see if it is correct.

Shapes and Sounds

CONSONANT CLASS	NO TONE MARKS x + Long vowel with no final consonant, or, Any vowel with a final nasal or semi vowel consonant, or, Special vowel	TONE MARKS		FINAL STOPS (can't have standard tone marks)	
		x́	x̆	x + ຈ, ດ, ບ Long vowels with final stop consonant	x + Short vowel with no final consonant (glottal stop), or, Short vowel with final stop consonant
HCC	4 ⌣	2 —	6 ⌢	6 ⌢	7 ⌡
MCC	1 _	2 —	5 ⌒	6 ⌢	7 ⌡
LCC	3 —	2 —	5 ⌒	5 ⌢	8 ⌢

The chart on the next page is the same as the chart above with syllable examples for each of the categories. In this chart the consonants ກ, ຂ, and ຄ are used and the vowels xາ and xະ. The final nasal ງ is used in some examples, but the other two final nasals, ນ and ມ, could also be interchanged with ງ. Similarly, the final semi-vowel ຍ is used in some examples, but the other final semi-vowel ວ could also be used in its place. Finally, the special vowel ເx is used in some examples, but the special vowels ແx, ເxາ, and xໍ could also be interchanged with ເx. This may help you get a better understanding for what tones are on what kinds of words.

Shapes and Sounds

CONSONANT CLASS	NO TONE MARKS x + Long vowel with no final consonant, or, Any vowel with a final nasal or semi vowel consonant, or, Special vowel		TONE MARKS x́		x̃		FINAL STOPS (can't have standard tone marks) x + ກ,ດ,ບ Long vowels with final stop consonant		x + Short vowel with no final consonant (glottal stop), or, Short vowel with final stop consonant	
HCC	◡ ຂາ ຂາງ ຂາຍ	4 ຂົງ ໄຂ	─ ຂ່າ ຂ່າງ ຂ່າຍ	2 ຂົ່ງ ໄຂ່	⌒ ຂ້າ ຂ້າງ ຂ້າຍ	6 ຂົ້ງ ໄຂ້	⌒ ຂາກ ຂາດ ຂາບ	6	⌒ ຂະ ຂັດ	7 ຂັກ ຂັບ
MCC	─ ກາ ກາງ ກາຍ	1 ກັງ ໄກ	─ ກ່າ ກ່າງ ກ່າຍ	2 ກັ່ງ ໄກ່	⌒ ກ້າ ກ້າງ ກ້າຍ	5 ກັ້ງ ໄກ້	⌒ ກາກ ກາດ ກາບ	5	◡ ກະ ກັດ	7 ກັກ ກັບ
LCC	─ ຄາ ຄາງ ຄາຍ	3 ຄັງ ໄຄ	─ ຄ່າ ຄ່າງ ຄ່າຍ	2 ຄັ່ງ ໄຄ່	⌒ ຄ້າ ຄ້າງ ຄ້າຍ	5 ຄັ້ງ ໄຄ້	⌒ ຄາກ ຄາດ ຄາບ	5	⌒ ຄະ ຄັດ	8 ຄັກ ຄັບ

5.5 Tone Mark Placement

Tone marks are always written over the initial consonant, not the vowel. However, don't be surprised if you meet some Lao people who don't know this rule. Often they will place the tone mark over the middle of the word, even if the middle character is a vowel. That is not correct.

Shapes and Sounds

In the case of a word with an initial consonant that has two symbols, such as ຫນ້າ, or ກວ່າ (special ວ case), the tone mark should be placed over the second symbol.

ຫນ້າ ກວ່າ
face more

Be careful not to confuse the symbols ວ and ອ with consonants when they appear as vowels in words. The tone mark should not be written over them, but over the consonant that precedes them.

ດ້ວຍ ຂ້ອຍ
with   I, my

5.6 Recognizing Tones

Look at the series of words below. Using the Lao tone rules from the chart above, and the numbers of the eight (nine!) Lao tones, place the tone number of each word in the blanks below. Practice pronouncing them aloud as you do them.

T 53 1. ຄາ   ຄ່າ   ຄ້າ

T 54 2. ຂາ   ຂ່າ   ຂ້າ

T 55 3. ກາ   ກ່າ   ກ້າ   ກ໊າ   ກໍາ

T 56 4. ຄາ   ຄ້າ   ຄາດ

T 57 5. ຂາ   ຂ້າ   ຂາດ

T 58 6. ກາ   ກ້າ   ກາດ

T 59 7. ຄາດ   ຂາດ   ກາດ

Shapes and Sounds

Now, look at the short story below. Each syllable has been separated (normally there are not spaces between syllables or words in Lao) so that you can more easily recognize the tone. Place the number of the tone in the blank below each word.

T 60

ถ้ำ   ที่ງ   ມີ   ຍິງ   ຂະ   ลา   ถิบ   ที่ງ   ถำ
—   —   —   —   —   —   —   —   —

ລົງ   ຂີ   ວິດ   ຢູ່   ແຫ່ງ   ທີ່ງ.   ລາວ   ມີ   ລา
—   —   —   —   —   —   —   —   —

ສອງ   ໂຕ.   ທຸກໆ   ເຊົ້າ   ລາວ   ຈູງ   ລา   ຢ່າງ   ຕາມ
—   —   —   —   —   —   —   —   —

ຖະ   ຫນົນ   ເພື່ອ   ໄປ   ສູ່   ທີ່ງ   ນາ.   ເຂົາ   ມີ
—   —   —   —   —   —   —   —   —

ທີ່ງ   ຂາຍ   ຫນຸ່ມ   ສອງ   ຄົນ   ເຫັນ   ຍິງ   ເຖົ້າ   ຄົນ
—   —   —   —   —   —   —   —   —

ນັ້ນ   ກັບ   ລา   ຂອງ   ລາວ   ແລະ   ຮ້ອງ   ຂຶ້ນ   ວ່າ:
—   —   —   —   —   —   —   —   —

"ສະ   ບາຍ   ດີ   ແມ່   ລา!"
—   —   —   —   —

"ສະ   ບາຍ   ດີ   ລູກ   ຂາຍ   ທັງ   ສອງ,"   ຍິງ
—   —   —   —   —   —   —   —

ເຖົ້າ   ຄົນ   ນັ້ນ   ຕອບ   ແລະ   ຍິ້ມ   ໃສ່   ພວກເຂົາ.
—   —   —   —   —   —   —   —

63

Shapes and Sounds

ANSWER KEY

1. ຕາ 3   ຕ່າ 2   ຕ້າ 5

2. ຂາ 4   ຂ່າ 2   ຂ້າ 6

3. ກາ 1   ກ່າ 2   ກ້າ 5   ກ໊າ 9   ກ໋າ 4

4. ຕາ 3   ຕ້າ 5   ຕາດ 5

5. ຂາ 4   ຂ້າ 6   ຂາດ 6

6. ກາ 1   ກ້າ 5   ກາດ 6

7. ຕາດ 5   ຂາດ 6   ກາດ 6

ຄັ້ງ	ທັ່ງ	ມີ	ຍິງ	ຂະ	ລາ	ຕິນ	ທັ່ງ	ດຳ
5	2	3	3	8	3	3	2	1

ລົງ	ຊິ	ວິດ	ຢູ່	ແທ່ງ	ທັ່ງ	ລາວ	ມີ	ລາ
5	3	8	2	2	2	3	3	3

ສອງ	ໂຕ	ທຸກໆ	ເຊົ້າ	ລາວ	ຈູງ	ລາ	ຢ່າງ	ຕາມ
4	1	8	5	3	1	3	2	1

ຄະ	ນົບ	ເພື່ອ	ໄປ	ສູ່	ທັງ	ນາ	ເຂົ້າ	ນີ້
7	4	2	1	2	2	3	5	5

ທັງ ຂາຍ ໜຸ່ມ ສອງ ຄົນ ເທັນ ຍິງ ເຖົ້າ ຄົນ
2   3   2   4   3   4   3   6   3

ນັ້ນ ກັບ ລາ ຂອງ ລາວ ແລະ ຮ້ອງ ຂຶ້ນ ວ່າ:
5   7   3   4   3   8   5   6   2

ສະ ບາຍ ດີ ແມ່ ລາ!
7   1   1   2   3

ສະ ບາຍ ດີ ລູກ ຂາຍ ທັງ ສອງ, ຍິງ
7   1   1   5   3   3   4   3

ເຖົ້າ ຄົນ ນັ້ນ ຕອບ ແລະ ຍິ້ມ ໃສ່ ພວກ ເຂົາ.
6   3   5   6   8   5   2   5   4

NOTES

6
MEMORIZATION TRICKS

6.1 Alphabet Memorization Trick

A good way to remember the alphabet (although it is not necessary as long as you can recognize each character) is to divide the consonants into six groups as the following:

ກຂຄງ • ຈສຊຍ • ດຕຖທນ • ບປຜຝພຟມ • ຢລວຫ • ອຮ
  1   2   3   4   5   6

- Each group begins with a MCC.
- Each group ends with a nasal (the ຫ and ຮ are actually nasalized in Lao).
- HCC (rising tone) consonants come before LCC (high tone) consonants.
- The first group is the "k" group, the second the "s" group, the third the "t" group, and the fourth the "p" group. The fifth group is the approximates, and the final group catches the remaining two consonants.
- As you go through the first four groups, the point in your mouth where the sound is made moves closer to the front of your mouth with each group.

6.2 Consonant Class Memorization Trick

As discussed in Chapter 4, Lao consonants are divided up into these three categories:

HCC ຂ ສ ຖ ຜ ຝ ຫ
MCC ກ ຈ ດ ຕ ບ ປ ຢ ອ
LCC ຄ ງ ຊ ຍ ທ ນ ພ ຟ ມ ລ ວ ຮ

67

Shapes and Sounds

It is not necessary to be able to recite the consonants that belong to each class. It is more important to be able to identify the right class of the consonant when you see it. However, a good way to remember which consonants are High Class and which ones are Middle Class is to memorize the three following sentences:

MCC: ໄກ່ ແຈ້ ດຳ ຕີ ບໍ່ ເປັນ ຢ່າ ເອົາ

Word for word translation: chicken bantam black fight no is don't take
Rough translation: "The black bantam chicken doesn't know how to fight so don't take him."

The initial consonants in this phrase make up the eight Middle Class Consonants.

HCC: ເຂົ້າ ສາມ ຖົງ ໃຜ ຝາກ ໃຫ້

Word for word translation: rice three bag who send for
Rough translation: "Who sent three bags of rice?"

The initial consonants in this phrase make up the six High Class Consonants.

LCC: ຄວາຍ ງົວ ຊ້າງ ຍ່າງ ທາງ ນຳ ແພ ຟາດ ມື ລຸງ ວอນ ຮ້ອງ

Word for word translation: buffalo cow elephant walk way water cloth strike hand uncle Vǫn shout.
Rough translation: "The buffalo, cow and elephant walk along the water. The cloth strikes Uncle Vǫn's hand and he shouts."

The initial consonants in this phrase make up the twelve Low Class Consonants. This sentence in particular doesn't make much sense, but enough, perhaps, to help you remember the LCCs.

7
ACCOMPANYING AUDIO TEXT

Learning how to pronounce the sounds of Lao by reading about it in a book is a bit problematic. It is next to impossible to know exactly what something sounds like unless you hear it with your own ears. For this reason audio files are provided with this book so that the reader can also become a listener. Examples of Lao words from each chapter in this book are recorded by a native Lao speaker. There are also additional materials not highlighted in the text that appear in the audio files.

The advantage of the digital audio files is that you can store them on any MP-3 device and quickly select the track that you want to play. While having a Lao conversation partner is probably the best thing you can do to learn the Lao language, you probably cannot have your Lao friend repeat tones hundreds of times like you can with audio tracks.

This chapter includes all of the text for the audio so that you can read along as you listen. The text is divided up into sections that correlate to the chapters in which the text appears. Also, the track number in the audio files appears next to each text to make it convenient to jump directly to the part you wish to practice.

7.1 Chapter 1 Associated Text

T 01 Alphabet (Consonants)
Listen to the Lao consonants and repeat them with the audio. Take note of the three different tones used to pronounce consonants and try to memorize each consonant along with the correct pronunciation and tone.

ກ ຂ ຄ ງ ຈ ສ ຊ ຍ ດ ຕ ຖ ທ ນ ບ ປ ຜ ຝ ພ ຟ ມ ຍ ລ ວ ຫ ອ ຮ

Shapes and Sounds

T 02 Animals / Objects

Listen to the Lao consonants and their associated animal or object. Memorize each animal and object that corresponds to the consonants.

ກ	ໄກ່	gk	gkai (2)	chicken
ຂ	ໄຂ່	kh	khai (2)	egg
ຄ	ຄວາຍ	kh	khwāi (3)	buffalo
ງ	ງົວ	ng	ngōua (3)	cow
ຈ	ຈອກ	ch	chǫk (6)	glass
ສ	ເສືອ	s	sēua (4)	tiger
ຊ	ຊ້າງ	s	sāng (5)	elephant
ຍ	ຍຸງ	ny	nyoung (3)	mosquito
ດ	ເດັກ	d	dek (7)	child
ຕ	ຕາ	dt	dtā (1)	eyes
ຖ	ຖົງ	th	thong (4)	bag
ທ	ທຸງ	th	thoung (3)	flag
ນ	ນົກ	n	nok (8)	bird
ບ	ແບ້	b	bāe (5)	goat
ປ	ປາ	bp	bpā (1)	fish
ຜ	ເຜິ້ງ	ph	phueng (6)	bee
ຝ	ຝົນ	f	fon (3)	rain
ພ	ພູ	ph	phōu (3)	mountain
ຟ	ໄຟ	f	fai (3)	fire
ມ	ແມວ	m	māeo (3)	cat
ຍ	ຍາ	y	yā (1)	medicine
ລ	ລິງ	l	līng (3)	monkey

Shapes and Sounds

ວ	ວີ	v	vī (3)	fan
ຫ	ຫ່ານ	h	hān (2)	goose
ອ	ໂອ	silent	ō (1)	bowl
ຣ	ເຮືອນ	h	hēuan (3)	house

T 03 The Consonant ຣ (Old Lao)

There are a few examples of words that used to contain the ຣ (r). Some of these words have replaced the ຣ with a ລ (l), and some have just dropped the ຣ altogether. Listen to these just to be aware of some of the sounds you might hear from time to time.

ຣົດ	(car)	ໂຣກ	(disease)
ໂຣຫິດ	(blood)	ຣັດຖະບານ	(government)
ພຣະເຈົ້າ	(God)	ໂປຣຕີນ	(protein)
ປຣະທານ	(to give)	ຝຣັ່ງ	(French)

T 04 Aspirated and Unaspirated Consonants

Listen for the different pronunciations as you go across each row. Pay attention to the difference in aspiration.

ກ່າ   ຂ່າ
ຄ່າ   ຕ່າ   ທ່າ
ບ່າ   ປ່າ   ພ່າ

T 05 Unaspirated Soft (voiced) and Abrupt (unvoiced) Consonants

All of these consonants are unaspirated, but listen for the difference in pronunciation. The two columns on the right are pronounced with a more abrupt sound than the two columns on the left.

ດໍ   ດໍ   ຕໍ   ຕໍ
ດໍ   ດໍ   ຕໍ   ຕໍ
ບໍ   ບໍ   ປໍ   ປໍ
ບໍ   ບໍ   ປໍ   ປໍ

Shapes and Sounds

T 06 Aspirated and Unaspirated Consonants
Listen for the difference in pronunciation between the left two columns and the right two columns. The consonants on the right are aspirated.

ຕ   ຕ   ທ   ທ
ຕ   ຕ   ທ   ທ
ປ   ປ   ພ   ພ
ປ   ປ   ພ   ພ

T 07 The Consonant ຈ
Listen to these examples of words with the consonant ຈ. The sound of ຈ is in between the sounds of "j" and "ch" in English.

ຈັບ	(to grab/hold/arrest)	ຈາກ	(from)
ຈ້າງ	(to hire)	ຈ່າຍ	(to pay)
ຈານ	(plate)	ຈິງ	(true)
ຈື່	(to remember)	ຈູບ	(to kiss)
ເຈັບ	(sick, ache)	ແຈ້ງ	(clear, to inform)
ໂຈນ	(thief)	ຈອງ	(to reserve)
ໃຈ	(heart, mind)	ເຈົ້າ	(yes, you)

T 08 The Consonant ງ
Listen to these words that begin with the consonant ງ (ng). Try to pronounce them as you listen.

ເງິນ	(silver, money)	ງ່າຍ	(easy)
ງານ	(work, party)	ເງົາ	(shadow)
ງູ	(snake)	ງາມ	(beautiful)
ງົວ	(cow)	ໂງ່	(stupid)

Shapes and Sounds

T 09 Final Stops
Here are examples of the three final stop consonants. Listen to the sound of each and note the position of your tongue and lips at the end of each word.

ການ   ກາດ   ກາບ
ບິກ   ບິດ   ບິບ
ດູກ   ດູດ   ດູບ

T 10 Final Nasals
Here are examples of the three final nasal consonants. Listen to the sound of each and note the position of your tongue and lips at the end of each word.

ກາງ   ການ   ກາມ
ບິງ   ບິນ   ບິມ
ດູງ   ດູນ   ດູມ

T 11 Special ວ Case
These are real words that employ the special usage of ວ. Remember that ວ in these examples is considered a consonant, not a vowel, and is comparable with the sound of the English consonant "w" before the vowel.

ກວ່າ   (more)   ກວາງ   (deer)
ກວ້າງຂວາງ (wide, large)   ແຂວງ   (province)
ຄວາຍ   (buffalo)   ຄວາມ   (makes an adj. a noun)
ຂວາ   (right—opp. of left)

T 12 Special ວ Case compared with the vowel ົວ
Note the difference in pronunciation between these pairs of words.

ກົ້ວ   ກວ່າ
ກົວງ   ກວາງ
ກົ້ວງຂົວງ   ກວ້າງຂວາງ
ຂົ້ວ   ຂວາ

Shapes and Sounds

ດອຍ   ດວາຍ
ດອມ   ດວາມ

T 13 Lao Numbers 0-10

The symbols in the left column are Lao numbers. Listen to the names of each of the numbers below. Try to memorize the Lao symbols when you hear the corresponding number being pronounced.

໐	ສູນ	0	໖	ຫົກ	6
໑	ຫນຶ່ງ	1	໗	ເຈັດ	7
໒	ສອງ	2	໘	ແປດ	8
໓	ສາມ	3	໙	ເກົ້າ	9
໔	ສີ່	4	໑໐	ສິບ	10
໕	ຫ້າ	5			

T 14 Lao Numbers 10s, 20s, 30s

These are examples of Lao numbers in the 10s, 20s and 30s. Listen and discover the pattern for saying any number.

໑໑	ສິບເອັດ	11
໑໒	ສິບສອງ	12
໑໓	ສິບສາມ	13
໑໔	ສິບສີ່	14
໑໕	ສິບຫ້າ	15
໒໐	ຊາວ	20
໒໑	ຊາວເອັດ	21
໒໒	ຊາວສອງ	22
໒໓	ຊາວສາມ	23
໓໐	ສາມສິບ	30
໓໑	ສາມສິບເອັດ	31
໓໒	ສາມສິບສອງ	32
໓໓	ສາມສິບສາມ	33

Shapes and Sounds

T 15 Lao Numbers 100 to 1,000,000

These are the names of each numeric category from 100 to 1,000,000.

໑୦୦	ຮ້ອຍ	100
໑.୦୦୦	ພັນ	1,000
໑୦.୦୦୦	ໝື່ນ	10,000
໑୦୦.୦୦୦	ແສນ	100,000
໑.୦୦୦.୦୦୦	ລ້ານ	1,000,000

T 16 Lao Numbers—multiple digits

These are some random numbers. Listen to how they are spoken in Lao.

๒๕๓	ສອງຮ້ອຍຫ້າສິບສາມ	253
໑໙໘๖	ພັນເກົ້າຮ້ອຍແປດສິບຫົກ	1,986
๓๕.୦୦୦	ສາມໝື່ນຫ້າພັນ ຫລື (or) ສາມສິບຫ້າພັນ	35,000
๗๖๔.୦୦୦	ເຈັດແສນຫົກໝື່ນສີ່ພັນ ຫລື (or) ເຈັດຮ້ອຍຫົກສິບສີ່ພັນ	764,000
๕.๕๔๒.໑໘໑	ຫ້າລ້ານຫ້າແສນສີ່ໝື່ນສອງພັນໜຶ່ງຮ້ອຍແປດສິບເອັດ ຫລື (or) ຫ້າລ້ານຫ້າຮ້ອຍສີ່ສິບສອງພັນໜຶ່ງຮ້ອຍແປດສິບເອັດ	5,542,181

7.2 Chapter 2 Associated Text

T 17 Vowels

Listen to the sounds of the Lao vowels. Repeat them along with the audio as you practice. Note that the short vowels (left column) end with a glottal stop and are spoken as short as possible.

Xະ	Xາ
X̊	X̊
X̂	X̂

Shapes and Sounds

ຂຸ   ຂຸ
ເXະ   ເX
ແXະ   ແX
ໂXະ   ໂX
ເXາະ   Xໍ
ເX̂   ເX̂
ເXັຍ   ເXຍ
ເXື̂ອ   ເXື̂ອ
X̂ວະ   X̂ວ

T 18 Special Vowels
Listen to the sounds of the special vowels. Pronounce them along with the audio as you practice. Notice that ໄX and ໃX are pronounced identically (Vientiane dialect).

ໄX   ໃX   ເX̂າ   Xຳ

T 19 Mixed Vowels
Listen to the sounds of the mixed vowels. The vowels that are in italics are very rare in common Lao. Listen to them to be aware of them, but don't worry about memorizing them.

ໄX	Xາຍ	*ເX̌ຍ*	ໂXຍ
ເX̂າ	Xາວ	*ເX̌ອ*	ໂXອ
X̂ວ	*X̌ວ*	*X̌ອຍ*	Xອຍ
X̂ຍ	*X̌ຍ*	*ເX̌ຍ*	ເX̌ຍ
X̂ອ	*X̌ອ*	*ເX̂ອ*	ເX̂ອ
Xຸຍ	*Xຸ̌ຍ*	*X̌ຳອ*	XຳອV
ເX̌ອ	ເXວ	*ເX̂ອຍ*	ເX̂ອຍ
ແX̌ອ	ແXວ	*X̌ອຍ*	Xອຍ

Shapes and Sounds

T 20 Common Mixed Vowels

These are the mixed vowels that are very common in Lao. All of them besides the second row are long vowels. Listen to the sounds and practice pronouncing them.

ꪙꪱꪥ   ꪙꪱꪫ

ꪙ꪿ꪫ   ꪈꪥ

ເꪙꪫ   ແꪙꪫ

ໂꪙꪥ   ꪙꪮꪥ

ເꪙ꪿ꪥ   ꪙຽꪫ

ເꪙ꪿ꪮꪥ   ꪙꪫꪥ

T 21 Short and Long Vowel Comparison

Here are examples of syllables that differ only by short and long vowels. The last three lines, syllables with final stops, also differ by tones as a result. Listen to them and practice pronouncing them, taking note of the difference in vowel length.

ອັມ	ອາມ	ຄັມ	ຄາມ
ອິມ	ອີມ	ຄິມ	ຄີມ
ອຸມ	ໂອມ	ຄຸມ	ໂຄມ
ອັກ	ອາກ	ຄັກ	ຄາກ
ອິກ	ອີກ	ຄິກ	ຄີກ
ອຸກ	ໂອກ	ຄຸກ	ໂຄກ

T 22 Short Vowels

Here are examples of syllables with short vowels. The first column consists of syllables with no final consonants and therefore glottal stops. The second column has final nasals, and the third column has a final stop consonant. Practice saying these syllables by pronouncing the vowels as short as possible.

ຄະ	ຄັມ	ຄັກ
ໂຄະ	ຄິມ	ຄິກ

77

Shapes and Sounds

ຈິ ຈິງ ຈິບ

ຊຸ ຊຸມ ຊຸດ

T 23 Long Vowels

Here are examples of syllables with long vowels. From left to right they end with no final consonant, a final nasal and a final stop. Listen closely to how long the vowel is pronounced and practice pronouncing them.

ຕາ ຕານ ຕາງ
ໂຕ ໂຕນ ໂຕງ
ຈີ ຈີງ ຈີບ
ຊູ ຊູມ ຊູດ

T 24 Comparison of the vowels X̃, X̣, and ເX̃.

Listen to the differences between these vowel sounds and practice pronouncing them.

ຕິ	ຕຶ	ເຕິ
ຂິ	ຂຶ	ເຂິ
ກິ	ກຶ	ເກິ
ບິ	ບຶ	ເບິ
ລິ	ລຶ	ເລິ
ຍິ	ຍຶ	ເຍິ

T 25 Comparison of the vowels ເX and ແX.

Listen to the differences between these vowel sounds and practice pronouncing them. Notice how the vowel sound changes slightly when shortened and spoken with a final consonant.

ເຕ	ແຕ	ເຕັດ	ແຕັດ
ເຂ	ແຂ	ເຂັບ	ແຂັບ
ເກ	ແກ	ເກັງ	ແກັງ
ເບ	ແບ	ເບັດ	ແບັດ

ເລ   ແລ   ເລັບ   ແລັບ
ເຮ   ແຮ   ເຮັກ   ແຮັກ

T 26 Comparison of the vowels ໄX and Xໍ.

Listen to the difference between these vowel sounds and practice pronouncing them.

ໄຄ   ຄໍ
ໄຂ   ຂໍ
ໄຄ   ຄໍ
ໄບ   ບໍ
ໄລ   ລໍ
ໄຮ   ຮໍ

T 27 Comparison of the vowels ເXຍ, ເXືອ, and Xົວ.

Listen to the difference between these vowel sounds and practice pronouncing them.

ເຄຍ   ເຄືອ   ຄົວ
ເຂຍ   ເຂືອ   ຂົວ
ເຄຍ   ເຄືອ   ຄົວ
ເບຍ   ເບືອ   ບົວ
ເລຍ   ເລືອ   ລົວ
ເຮຍ   ເຮືອ   ຮົວ

7.3 Chapter 3 Associated Text

T 28 Basic Tones (1-6)

Listen to these examples of the six basic tones in Lao. Note the contour of the sound as well as the pitch. Try to pronounce them identically to the audio.

ກາ (1)   ຄ່າ (2)   ຄາ (3)   ຂາ (4)   ຄ້າ (5)   ຂ້າ (6)
crow   value   syllable leg   to trade to kill

T 29 Tones 7 and 8

Listen to these words with Tones 7 and 8. Listen very carefully to hear the "rising" of Tone 7 and the slight "falling" of Tone 8. Practice pronouncing them along with the audio.

ກັດ(7)   ັດ(8)   ຂັດ(7)
to bite   to copy   syllable

T 30 Tone 9 X̃

Here are examples of tones with all the different tone marks on one word. The only new tone is Tone 9, on the fourth word. Note its unique contour. However, don't worry about mastering Tone 9, as it is rare in common Lao.

ແປນ(1)   ແປ່ນ(2)   ແປ້ນ(5)   ແປ໊ນ(9)   ແປ໋ນ(4)

T 31 Tones on Short Vowels

Listen to these words with short vowels and final nasals or semi-vowels, and special vowels. Notice how the tone is mostly pronounced "through" the final nasal or final vowel sound and how the initial vowel sound is still kept as short as possible.

ໄກ(1)   ໄກ່(2)   ໃກ້(5)
far   chicken   near

ເຂົາ(3)   ເຂົ່າ(2)   ເຂົ້າ(5)   ເສົາ(4)   ເສົ້າ(6)
to stop   to rent   morning   column   sad

ນັງ(3)   ນັ່ງ(2)   ນັ້ງ(5)   ໜັງ(4)   ໜັ້ງ(6)
syllable   to sit   syllable   skin   syllable

ຄັນ(3)   ຄັ່ນ(2)   ຄັ້ນ(5)   ຂັນ(4)   ຂັ້ນ(6)
to scratch   to score cloth   to knead   to crow   step

T 32 Tones on Final Particles

Listen to the tone shift on some of the final particles below. For now, just be aware that this "shift" exists. Later you can memorize which words are spoken with which tones (exceptions to the tone rules) to speak them correctly.

Shapes and Sounds

Sentence	Written Tone #	Actual Tone
ເຊີນກິນເລີຍ! Please eat!	3	3
ເຈົ້າຢາກໄດ້ກໍເອົາສາ! You would like this; go ahead and take it!	4	4
ເຈົ້າຊິໄປຫລວງພະບາງບໍ? Are you going to go to Luang Prabang	1	4
ເຊີນລາວເຂົ້າມາແມ! Invite him in!	3	5
ລາວກໍເປັນຄົນດີຢູ່ນາ! He is a pretty good person!	3	5
ແມ່ນຄວາມລາວເວົ້າຕິ! It is as he says (uncertain)!	1	5
ມ່ວນແທ້ນໍ! This is very fun!	3	5
ຂອບໃຈເດີ! Thank you!	1	5

T 33 **Phrase 1 Ideal**
Listen to the ideal pronunciation of tones in a Lao sentence.

ຂ້ອຍຮຽນພາສາລາວຢູ່ດົງໂດກ
I learn the Lao language at Dong Dok.

T 34 **Phrase 1 Ordinary**
Listen to the pronunciation of a Lao sentence spoken in a more ordinary way. Note the rhythm and the tones in the sentence. Practice saying the phrase along with the audio.

ຂ້ອຍຮຽນພາສາລາວຢູ່ດົງໂດກ
I learn the Lao language at Dong Dok.

Shapes and Sounds

T 35 Phrase 2 Ideal
Listen to the ideal pronunciation of tones in a Lao sentence.

ຂ້ອຍມັກຫລິ້ນກິລາເຕະບານ.

I like to play soccer.

T 36 Phrase 2 Ordinary
Listen to the pronunciation of a Lao sentence spoken in a more ordinary way. Note the rhythm and the tones in the sentence. Practice saying the phrase along with the audio.

ຂ້ອຍມັກຫລິ້ນກິລາເຕະບານ.

I like to play soccer.

T 37 Phrase 3 Ideal
Listen to the ideal pronunciation of tones in a Lao sentence.

ຮ້ານອາຫານຮ້ານນີ້ຂາຍເຄື່ອງກິນດື່ມ.

This restaurant sells food and drinks.

T 38 Phrase 3 Ordinary
Listen to the pronunciation of a Lao sentence spoke in a more ordinary way. Note the rhythm and the tones in the sentence. Practice saying the phrase along with the audio.

ຮ້ານອາຫານຮ້ານນີ້ຂາຍເຄື່ອງກິນດື່ມ.

This restaurant sells food and drinks.

T 39 Phrase 4 Ideal
Listen to the ideal pronunciation of tones in a Lao sentence.

ອ້າຍຂ້ອຍຊິໄປຕະຫລາດແລງເພື່ອຊື້ອາຫານ.

My older brother will go to the evening market to buy food.

T 40 Phrase 4 Ordinary
Listen to the pronunciation of a Lao sentence spoken in a more ordinary way. Note the rhythm and the tones in the sentence. Practice saying the phrase along with the audio.

ອ້າຍຂ້ອຍຊິໄປຕະຫລາດແລງເພື່ອຊື້ອາຫານ.

My older brother will go to the evening market to buy food.

T 41 Phrase 5 Ideal
Listen to the ideal pronunciation of tones in a Lao sentence.

ເຈົ້າກິນເຂົ້າແລ້ວບໍ?

Have you eaten yet?

T 42 Phrase 5 Ordinary
Listen to the pronunciation of a Lao sentence spoken in a more ordinary way. Note the rhythm and the tones in the sentence. Practice saying the phrase along with the audio.

ເຈົ້າກິນເຂົ້າແລ້ວບໍ?

Have you eaten yet?

7.4 Chapter 4 Associated Text

T 43 Tone Practice (Tones 1-6)
Listen to the six basic tones in these real Lao words and syllables and practice pronouncing them.

gkao (1)	gkao (2)	khao (3)	khao (4)	gkao (5)	khao (6)
ເກາ	ເກ່າ	ເຄາ	ເຂາ	ເກົ້າ	ເຂົ້າ
to scratch	old	syllable	horn	nine	rice

T 44 Tone Practice (Tones 1-6)
Listen to the six basic tones in these real Lao words and syllables and practice pronouncing them.

gkā (1)	khā (2)	khā (3)	khā (4)	khā (5)	khā (6)
ກາ	ຄ່າ	ຄາ	ຂາ	ຄ້າ	ຂ້າ
crow	value	syllable	leg	to trade	to kill

T 45 Tone Practice (Tones 2-6)
Listen to Tones 2-6 in these real Lao words and practice pronouncing them.

sao (2)	sao (3)	sao (4)	sao (5)	sao (6)
ເຊົ່າ	ເຊາ	ເສາ	ເຊົ້າ	ເສົ້າ
to rent	to stop	column	morning	sad

Shapes and Sounds

T 46 Tone Practice (Tones 2, 4, 5 and 6)
Listen to Tones 2, 4, 5 and 6 in these real Lao words and practice pronouncing them.

mai (2)	mai (4)	mai (5)	mai (6)
ໃໝ່	ໃໝ	ໄມ້	ໃໝ້
new	silk	wood	to burn

T 47 Tone Practice (Tones 2-5)
Listen to Tones 2-5 in these real Lao words and practice pronouncing them.

mā (2)	mā (3)	mā (4)	mā (5)
ໝ່າ	ມາ	ໝາ	ມ້າ
to soak	to come	dog	horse

T 48 Tone Practice (Tones 2-6 on "nang" and "nāng")
Listen to all the different possible tones (2-6) on the syllables "nang" and "nāng". Listen carefully to be able to distinguish the different sounds. Practice pronouncing them along with the audio.

ນັງ ນັ່ງ ນັ້ງ
ໜັງ ໜັ່ງ ໜັ້ງ
ນາງ ນ່າງ ນ້າງ
ໜາງ ໜ່າງ ໜ້າງ

T 49 Tone Practice (Tones 7 and 8)
Listen to Tones 7 and 8 on the syllables below. Listen carefully to be able to distinguish the different sounds. Practice pronouncing them along with the audio.

ດັດ   ຄະ   ຂັດ   ຂະ   ກັດ   ກະ

T 50 Tone Practice (Tone 3 / 1 and 2)
The first four pairs of words here contrast Tone 3 with Tone 2. The last two pairs contrast Tone 1 with Tone 2. Listen carefully to be able to distinguish them. Practice pronouncing them along with the audio.

Shapes and Sounds

ນັງ	ນັ່ງ
syllable	to sit

ມາ	ໝ່າ
to come	to soak

ເຊົາ	ເຊົ່າ
to stop	to rent

ຄາ	ຄ່າ
syllable	value

ຈິງ	ຈິ່ງ
true	syllable

ກຽວ	ກ່ຽວ
coil	concerning

T 51 Tone Practice (Tones 5 and 6)

These pairs of words contrast Tone 5 with Tone 6. Listen carefully to be able to distinguish them. Practice pronouncing them along with the audio.

ຊ້າ	ສ້າ
slow	type of tree

ຄ້າ	ຂ້າ
to trade	to kill

ເທິ້າ	ເຖົ້າ
lean against	old

ເຊົ້າ	ເສົ້າ
morning	sad

ຄອບ	ຂອບ
syllable	edge

ຊາດ	ສາດ
nation	mat

T 52 Tone Practice (Tones 8 and 7)

These pairs of words contrast Tone 8 with Tone 7. Listen carefully to be able to distinguish them. Practice pronouncing them along with the audio.

ຮັກ	ຫັກ
to love	to break

ເຮັດ	ເຫັດ
to do, to make	mushroom

ວັດ	ຫວັດ
temple	cold (sickness)

ພັກ	ຜັກ
to rest	vegetable

ພິດ	ຜິດ
poison	wrong

ຊຸດ	ສຸດ
set	end

ມົດ	ຫມົດ
ant	finished, all

7.5 Chapter 5 Associated Text

T 53 Tone Marks on LCC

Listen to the different tones on Low Class Consonants. Practice pronouncing them along with the audio.

ຄາ   ຄ່າ   ຄ້າ

T 54 Tone Marks on HCC

Listen to the different tones on High Class Consonants. Practice pronouncing them along with the audio.

ຂາ   ຂ່າ   ຂ້າ

T 55 Tone Marks on MCC
Listen to the different tones on Middle Class Consonants. Practice pronouncing them along with the audio.

ກາ   ກ່າ   ກ້າ   ກ໊າ   ກ໋າ

T 56 LCC X̌ and Final Stop Comparison
Listen to the "natural" tone of a Low Class Consonant in the first example, the tone with X̌ in the second example, and the tone with a final stop in the last example. Note that the tone is the same in the last two. Practice pronouncing them along with the audio.

ຄາ   ຄ້າ   ຄາດ

T 57 HCC X̌ and Final Stop Comparison
Listen to the "natural" tone of a High Class Consonant in the first example, the tone with X̌ in the second example, and the tone with a final stop in the last example. Note that the tone is the same in the last two. Practice pronouncing them along with the audio.

ຂາ   ຂ້າ   ຂາດ

T 58 MCC X̌ and Final Stop Comparison
Listen to the "natural" tone of a Middle Class Consonant in the first example, the tone with X̌ in the second example, and the tone with a final stop in the last example. Note that the tones are <u>different</u> in the last two, unlike LCCs and HCCs. Practice pronouncing them along with the audio.

ກາ   ກ້າ   ກາດ

T 59 Final Stops on LCC, HCC and MCC
Listen to the tones on these syllables with final stops, one from each consonant class. Note the difference and practice pronouncing them along with the audio.

ຄາດ   ຂາດ   ກາດ

Shapes and Sounds

T 60 Mother of Donkeys Story ແມ່ລາ

Listen to this story in Lao. Try to get a feel for the rhythm and tones and how they are pronounced in normal speech. As you progress in your ability to read Lao, read this story out loud along with the audio.

ຄັ້ງໜຶ່ງ ມີຍິງຊະລາຄົນໜຶ່ງກຳລັງຊີວິດຢູ່ແຫ່ງໜຶ່ງ. ລາວມີ ລາສອງໂຕ. ທຸກາງເຊົ້າລາວຈູງລາຢ່າງຕາມຖະໜົນ ເພື່ອໄປສູ່ທົ່ງນາ. ເຊົ້າມື້ໜຶ່ງຊາຍໜຸ່ມສອງຄົນເຫັນຍິງເຖົ້າຄົນນັ້ນກັບລາຂອງລາວ ແລະ ຮ້ອງຂຶ້ນວ່າ, "ສະບາຍດີແມ່ລາ!"

"ສະບາຍດີລູກຊາຍທັງສອງ," ຍິງເຖົ້າຄົນນັ້ນຕອບ ແລະຍິ້ມໃສ່ພວກເຂົາ.

Once there lived an old woman. She had two donkeys. Every morning she went with them down the street to the fields. One morning two young men saw the old woman with her donkeys and shouted, "Good morning, mother of donkeys!"

"Good morning, my sons," the old woman answered and smiled at them.

7.6 Graded Reading and Listening Material

Tracks 61-78 below contain short sentences for simple reading and listening practice.[1] These series of sentences are good for Lao learners as they slowly build on a basic vocabulary and do not lose the beginning student with too many new terms. Listen to these sentences in the audio to get a feel for the sound and rhythm of the Lao language. Then practice reading along with the audio and trying to pronounce the phrases correctly.

---

[1] This material is taken from the "Lao Language for J.O.C.V. Volunteers" text published for a three-week course for Japanese volunteers at the National University of Laos. Some of the material has been updated and modified to better represent an English speaking audience and current dates and prices. The English transliterations in the right columns are new with this text.

Shapes and Sounds

T 61 What color is the pencil? ສຳສີຫຍັງ?

1.	ນີ້ແມ່ນຫຍັງ?	What is this?
2.	ນີ້ແມ່ນສໍສີ.	This is a colored pencil.
3.	ນີ້ແມ່ນສໍສີຫຍັງ?	What color is this pencil?
4.	ນີ້ແມ່ນສໍສີແດງ	This is a red pencil.
5.	ນັ້ນແມ່ນຫຍັງ?	What is that?
6.	ນັ້ນແມ່ນສໍສີດຳ	That is a black pencil.
7.	ນັ້ນແມ່ນສໍສີຫຍັງ?	What color is that pencil?
8.	ນັ້ນແມ່ນສໍສີຂຽວ.	That is a green pencil.
9.	ນີ້ແມ່ນສໍສີຫຍັງ ກັບສໍສີຫຍັງ?	This pencil with this pencil are what colors?
10.	ນັ້ນແມ່ນສໍສີແດງ ກັບສໍສີດຳ	That is a red pencil and a black pencil.
11.	ພຸ້ນແມ່ນສໍສີຂຽວ ກັບສໍສີຫຍັງ?	That is a green pencil with what color of a pencil?
12.	ຂໍສີຂຽວຫນຶ່ງອັນແດ່?	May I have one green pencil, please?
13.	ຂໍສີຂຽວຫນຶ່ງອັນ ກັບສໍສີເຫຼືອງສອງອັນ?	May I have one green pencil and two yellow pencils?
14.	ເຊີນເອົາສໍສີເຫຼືອງສອງອັນ	Please take two yellow pencils.
15.	ເຊີນວາງສໍສີເຫຼືອງສອງອັນ	Please put two yellow pencils (on the table).
16.	ເຊີນເອົາສໍສີບົວສາມອັນ	Please take three pink pencils.
17.	ຂໍສີບົວສາມອັນ ກັບສໍສີນ້ຳຕານສອງອັນ?	May I have three pink pencils and two brown pencils?

89

Shapes and Sounds

18.	ຂອບໃຈ.	Thank you.
19.	ບໍ່ເປັນຫຍັງ.	You're welcome.

T 62 How Many? How Much? ຈັກອັນ? ຈັກກີບ?

1. ຢູ່ນີ້ມີສໍສີຈັກອັນ? — How many pencils are there here?
2. ຢູ່ນັ້ນມີສໍສີສີ່ອັນ. — There are four pencils there.
3. ເຊີນເອົາສໍສີຟ້າ. — Please take the blue pencil.
4. ຂ້ອຍເອົາສໍສີຟ້າຈັກອັນ? — How many blue pencils (may) I take?
5. ເຈົ້າເອົາສໍສີຟ້າ ໕ ອັນ. — You (may) take five blue pencils.
6. ເຈົ້າມີສໍສີຫຍັງ? — What color of pencil do you have?
7. ຂ້ອຍມີສໍສີຂຽວອ່ອນ. — I have a light green pencil.
8. ເຈົ້າມີສໍສີຂຽວອ່ອນຈັກອັນ? — How many light green pencils do you have?
9. ຂ້ອຍມີສໍສີຂຽວອ່ອນສາມອັນ. — I have three light green pencils.
10. ເຈົ້າມີສໍສີນ້ຳຕານບໍ? — Do you have a brown pencil?
11. ມີ. — I do.
12. ເຈົ້າມີສໍສີຂຽວບໍ? — Do you have a green pencil?
13. ບໍ່ມີ. ຂ້ອຍມີສໍສີມ່ວງ. — No, I don't have one. I have a purple pencil.
14. ເຈົ້າມີສໍສີມ່ວງຈັກອັນ? — How many purple pencils do you have?
15. ຂ້ອຍມີສໍສີມ່ວງຫ້າອັນ. — I have five purple pencils.

16. ອັນນີ້ຈັກກີບ?   How much is this? (Lit. "This thing how many Kip?)
17. ອັນນັ້ນ ໕.໐໐໐ ກີບ.   That is 5000 Kip.
18. ເຈົ້າມີເງິນຈັກກີບ?   How much money do you have?
19. ຂ້ອຍມີເງິນ ໑໐.໐໐໐ ກີບ.   I have 10,000 Kip.
20. ຂ້ອຍມີເງິນ ໒໐.໐໐໐ ກີບ.   I have 20,000 Kip.

T 63 What is Your Name? ເຈົ້າຊື່ຫຍັງ?

1. ສະບາຍດີ. ເຈົ້າຊື່ຫຍັງ?   Hello. What's your name?
2. ສະບາຍດີ. ຂ້ອຍຊື່ ເດວິດ ນາມສະກຸນ ເທເລີ.   Hello. My name is David, last name Taylor.
3. ເຈົ້າເດ?   And you?
4. ຂ້ອຍຊື່ ມາກ ນາມສະກຸນ ວິນລຽມ.   My name is Mark, last name William.
5. ຂ້ອຍຊື່ ແຈເນັດ ນາມສະກຸນ ຈອນສັນ.   My name is Janet, last name Johnson.
6. ອາຈານຊື່ຫຍັງ?   Professor, what is your name?
7. ຂ້ອຍຊື່ ສຸລິຍາ.   My name is Sou'li'nyā.
8. ອາຈານ ນາມສະກຸນ ຫຍັງ?   Professor, what is your last name?
9. ຂ້ອຍນາມສະກຸນ ໂຫລານຸພາບ.   My last name is Hōlānou'phāp.
10. ຂໍໂທດ. ເຈົ້າເຮັດວຽກຫຍັງ?   Excuse me. What is your job?
11. ຂ້ອຍເປັນ ນາງພະຍາບານ.   I am a nurse.

Shapes and Sounds

12.	ພວກເຈົ້າເດ?	And all of you?
13.	ພວກຂ້ອຍເປັນອາຈານສອນ.	We are all teachers.
14.	ພວກເຈົ້າສອນວິຊາຫຍັງ?	What subjects do all of you teach?
15.	ຂ້ອຍສອນວິຊາລ້ຽງສັດ.	I teach animal husbandry.
16.	ຂ້ອຍສອນວິຊາໄຟຟ້າ.	I teach electricity.
17.	ພວກເຈົ້າເຮັດວຽກຢູ່ໃສ?	Where do all of you work?
18.	ຂ້ອຍເຮັດວຽກຢູ່ໂຮງໝໍມະໂຫສົດ	I work at Ma'hōsot Hospital.
19.	ຂ້ອຍສອນຢູ່ໂຮງຮຽນກະເສດນາບົງ. ສ່ວນລາວສອນ ຢູ່ໂຮງຮຽນເອເລັກໂຕນິກ.	I teach at Nābong Agricultural School. He teaches at the Electronics school.
20.	ພວກເຮົາຮຽນພາສາລາວຢູ່ ມະຫາວິທະຍາໄລແຫ່ງຊາດ.	We study Lao at the National University.

T 64 Where do you go? ໄປໃສ?

1.	ສະບາຍດີ. ເຈົ້າຊິໄປໃສ?	Hello. Where are you going? (Lit. "Where will you go?")
2.	ສະບາຍດີ. ຂ້ອຍຊິໄປໂຮງໝໍ.	Hello. I am going to the hospital.
3.	ເຈົ້າເດ?	And you?
4.	ຂ້ອຍຊິໄປຕະຫຼາດ.	I am going to the market.
5.	ນາງ ແຈເນັດ ໄປໃສ?	Where is Miss Janet going?

6. ລາວໄປໂຮງຮຽນກະເສດນາບົງ. She is going to the Nābong Agricultural School.
7. ທ່ານ ເດວິດ ເດ? How about Mr. David?
8. ລາວໄປໂຮງຮຽນເອເລັກໂຕຣນິກ. He is going to the electronics school.
9. ນາງ ແຈເນັດ ແລະ ທ່ານເດວິດໄປສອນທັງສີ. Miss Janet and Mr. David go to teach.
10. ຕອນເຊົ້າພວກເຮົາໄປໂຮງຮຽນ. In the morning we go to school.
11. ຕອນທ່ຽງ ພວກເຮົາພັກ ແລະ ກິນເຂົ້າ. At noon we rest and have lunch.
12. ຕອນບ່າຍ ພວກເຮົາສອນອີກ. In the afternoon we teach again.
13. ຕອນແລງ ອາຈານເມືອເຮືອນ. In the evening the professor returns home.
14. ຕອນກາງຄືນ ເຈົ້າໄປໃສ? Where do you go at night?
15. ຕອນກາງຄືນ ຂ້ອຍໄປທ່ຽວ. At night I go out.
16. ຄົນຕ່າງປະເທດ ມາເຮັດຫຍັງຢູ່ລາວ. What do the foreigners come to do in Laos?
17. ພວກເຮົາມາເຮັດວຽກຊ່ອຍຄົນລາວ. We come to work to help the Lao people.
18. ຄົນຕ່າງປະເທດ ເຮັດວຽກຢູ່ແຂວງຕ່າງໆ ໃນປະເທດລາວ. Foreigners work in various provinces in Laos.
19. ຄົນຕ່າງປະເທດ ເຮັດວຽກຢູ່ ໃສອີກ? Where are other places that foreigners work?

Shapes and Sounds

20. ເຂົາເຈົ້າເຮັດວຽກຢູ່ອາຟະລິກາ ແລະອາເມລິກາລາຕິນນຳອີກ. — They also work in Africa and Latin America.

T 65 Going to a Restaurant ໄປຮ້ານອາຫານ

1. ເຈົ້າຫິວບໍ? — Are you hungry?
2. ຫິວ. — Yes, I am.
3. ພວກເຮົາໄປກິນເຂົ້າກັນເທາະ. — Let's go and eat.
4. ພວກເຮົາຊິໄປກິນເຂົ້າຢູ່ໃສ? — Where are we going to eat?
5. ພວກເຮົາໄປກິນເຂົ້າຢູ່ຮ້ານກິນດື່ມ. — We are going to eat at a restaurant.
6. ຮ້ານກິນດື່ມຢູ່ໃສ? — Where is the restaurant?
7. ຮ້ານກິນດື່ມຢູ່ໃກ້ຕະຫຼາດ. — The restaurant in near the market.
8. ເຈົ້າຊິກິນຫຍັງ? — What are you going to eat?
9. ຂ້ອຍຊິກິນເຝີ ກັບນ້ຳຫວານ. — I'm going to eat noodle soup and a soft drink.
10. ຂ້ອຍຊິກິນເຂົ້າຂົ້ວ ກັບໂອລຽງ. — I'm going to eat fried rice and Oliang.
11. ອາຈານກິນເຂົ້າໜຽວ, ລາບ ແລະແກງຈືດ. — The professor eats sticky rice, lāp and soup.
12. ລາວກິນເຂົ້າຈ້າວ, ແກງຈືດ ແລະຊາເຢັນ. — He eats steamed rice, soup and iced tea.
13. ເອົາເຂົ້າຂົ້ວໜຶ່ງຈານ ກັບນ້ຳຫວານໜຶ່ງແກ້ວໃຫ້ແດ່. — May I have one plate of fried rice and one bottle of a soft drink please?

14.	ເອົາເຝິທີ່ງຕ້ອຍ ກັບຊາ ເຢັນ ທີ່ງຈອກໃຫ້ແດ່.	May I have one bowl of noodle soup and one cup of iced tea, please?
15.	ເຂົ້າຂົ້ວຈານທີ່ງເທົ່າໃດ?	How much is one plate of fried rice?
16.	ເຂົ້າຂົ້ວຈານທີ່ງ ໑໓.000 ກີບ.	One plate of fried rice is 13,000 Kip.
17.	ຊາເຢັນຈອກທີ່ງ ໑.000 ກີບ.	One cup of iced tea is 1,000 Kip.
18.	ເກັບເງິນແດ່ເດີ.	Can we have the bill?
19.	ທັງໝົດເທົ່າໃດ?	How much for everything?
20.	ທັງໝົດ ໕໔.000 ກີບ.	All together it is 54,000 Kip.

T 66 At the Market ຢູ່ຕະຫຼາດ

1.	ຕະຫຼາດຢູ່ພຸ້ນ.	The market is over there.
2.	ຕະຫຼາດຢູ່ຕິດກັບວັດ.	The market is next to the temple.
3.	ຄົນລາວມັກໄປຕະຫຼາດ.	Lao people like to go to the market.
4.	ເຂົາເຈົ້າຊື້ຊີ້ນໝູ, ປາ ແລະໄກ່ ຢູ່ຕະຫຼາດ.	They buy pork, fish and chicken at the market.
5.	ຜັກ ແລະໝາກໄມ້ ຢູ່ຕະຫຼາດບໍ່ແພງ.	Vegetables and fruit at the market are not expensive.
6.	ເຂົາເຈົ້າຂາຍໝາກໄມ້ຢູ່ ໃສ?	Where do they sell fruit?
7.	ເຂົາເຈົ້າຂາຍໝາກໄມ້ ຢູ່ໜ້າຕະຫຼາດ.	They sell fruit in front of the market.
8.	ຮ້ານຂາຍເຂົ້າໜົມຢູ່ໃສ?	Where is the snack shop?

Shapes and Sounds

9. ຮ້ານຂາຍເຂົ້າໜົມຢູ່ໜ້າຕະຫຼາດ. — The snack shop is in front of the market.
10. ຢູ່ຕະຫຼາດ ມີຮ້ານຂາຍຊີ້ນ ແລະຮ້ານຂາຍຜັກ. — There are meat shops and vegetable shops at the market.
11. ຮ້ານຂາຍຊີ້ນ ຢູ່ໃນຕະຫຼາດ. — The meat shop is at the market.
12. ມີຮ້ານຂາຍເຝີ ຢູ່ໃນຕະຫຼາດຄືກັນ. — There is also a noodle shop at the market.
13. ຕະຫຼາດຢູ່ນີ້ນ້ອຍ. — The market here is small.
14. ຕະຫຼາດຢູ່ພຸ້ນໃຫຍ່. — The market over there is big.
15. ຜັກຢູ່ຕະຫຼາດຖືກ. — The vegetables in the market are cheap.
16. ອາຫານຢູ່ນີ້ຖືກ. — The food here is cheap.
17. ເຂົ້າໜົມຢູ່ຕະຫຼາດແຊບບໍ? — Do the snacks at the market taste good?
18. ແຊບຫຼາຍ. — Yes, they are very delicious.
19. ເດັກນ້ອຍມັກກິນເຂົ້າໜົມ. — Children like to eat snacks.
20. ຄົນລາວ ແລະຄົນອາເມລິກາ ມັກກິນເຂົ້າໜົມ. — Lao and American people like to eat snacks.

T 67 Buy—Sell   ຊື້-ຂາຍ

1. ໃຜຊື້ເສື້ອ? — Who buys the shirt?
2. ຂ້ອຍຊື້ເສື້ອ. — I buy the shirt.
3. ເຈົ້າຊື້ເສື້ອຈັກຜືນ? — How many shirts do you buy?
4. ຂ້ອຍຊື້ເສື້ອສອງຜືນ. — I buy two shirts.
5. ຂ້ອຍຊື້ໂສ້ງທີ່ງຜືນ. — I buy one pair of trousers.

Shapes and Sounds

6. ແມ່ຄ້າ ຂາຍຫຍັງ? — What does the saleswoman sell?
7. ຂ້ອຍຂາຍປີ້ງໄກ່. — I sell grilled chicken.
8. ປີ້ງໄກ່ ປີ້ງລະເທົ່າໃດ? — How much does one stick of grilled chicken cost?
9. ປີ້ງລະພັນ. — One thousand each.
10. ຂ້ອຍຊື້ປີ້ງໄກ່ສອງປີ້ງເດີ. — I buy two sticks of grilled chicken.
11. ຂ້ອຍຊື້ເຂົ້າໜຽວ ສາມຮ້ອຍກີບເດີ. — I will buy three hundred Kip (worth) of sticky rice, please.
12. ໃຜຊື້ເຂົ້າໜຽວກັບປີ້ງໄກ່? — Who buys sticky rice and grilled chicken?
13. ອາສາສະໝັກສອງຄົນ ຊື້ເຂົ້າໜຽວກັບປີ້ງໄກ່. — Two volunteers buy sticky rice and grilled chicken.
14. ອາສາສະໝັກຜູ້ຊາຍ ຊື້ແພຮໍໂປ້. — The male volunteers buy towels.
15. ອາສາສະໝັກແມ່ຍິງ ຊື້ ສິ້ນ. — The female volunteers buy Lao skirts.
16. ນີ້ແມ່ນແພຮໍໂປ້ຂອງໃຜ? — Whose towel is this?
17. ແພຮໍໂປ້ຂອງຂ້ອຍ. — The towel is mine.
18. ສິ້ນຂອງຂ້ອຍ. — The Lao skirt is mine.
19. ພໍ່ຄ້າກັບແມ່ຄ້າຂາຍເຄື່ອງ ຢູ່ໃນ ແລະຢູ່ນອກ ຕະຫຼາດ. — Salesmen and saleswomen sell things inside and outside of the market.
20. ເຂົາເຈົ້າຂາຍເສື້ອ, ໂສ້ງ, ແພຮໍໂປ້ ແລະ ສິ້ນ. — They sell shirts, trousers, towels and Lao skirts.

Shapes and Sounds

T 68 Bīa Mountain is the Highest   ພູເບັ້ຍສູງທີ່ສຸດ

1. ມື້ວານນີ້ເຈົ້າໄປທ່ຽວໃສ? — Where did you go touring yesterday?
2. ມື້ວານນີ້ຂ້ອຍໄປທ່ຽວຢູ່ເທິງພູ. — Yesterday I went touring on top of a mountain.
3. ພູຫຍັງ? — What mountain?
4. ພູເຂົາຄວາຍ. — Phōu Khao Khwāi. ("Buffalo Horn Mountain")
5. ສູງບໍ? — Is it high?
6. ສູງຫຼາຍ ແຕ່ພູໝຽງສູງກວ່າ. — It is very high but Mīang Mountain is higher.
7. ພູເບັ້ຍເດ? — How about Bīa Mountain?
8. ພູເບັ້ຍສູງກວ່າພູໝຽງ. — Bīa Mountain is higher than Mīang Mountain.
9. ພູເບັ້ຍສູງກວ່າໝູ່ບໍ? — Is Bīa Mountain the highest?
10. ພູເບັ້ຍສູງກວ່າໝູ່. — Bīa Mountain is the highest.
11. ພູເຂົາຄວາຍຢູ່ໃສ? — Where is Phōu Khao Khwāi?
12. ຢູ່ໃກ້ໆ ວຽງຈັນ. — Near Vientiane (Vīang Chan).
13. ເຈົ້າຮູ້ຈັກນ້ຳງື່ມບໍ? — Do you know Nam Ngēum?
14. ຮູ້ຈັກ, ນ້ຳງື່ມງາມຫຼາຍ. — Yes, I do. Nam Ngēum is very beautiful.
15. ນ້ຳງື່ມຍາວຈັກກິໂລແມັດ? — How many kilometres long is the Nam Ngēum river?
16. ບໍ່ຮູ້ຈັກປານໃດ. — I'm not sure.
17. ແມ່ນ້ຳຂອງຍາວປະມານ ໔,໒໐໐ ກິໂລແມັດ. — The Mekong river is about 4,200 kilometres long.

18. ແມ່ນ້ຳຂອງ ຍາວກວ່າ ແມ່ນ້ຳເຈົ້າພະຍາ. — The Mekong river is longer than the Chao Pha'nyā river.
19. ແມ່ນ້ຳນິນຍາວທີ່ສຸດໃນໂລກ. — The Nile is the longest river in the world.
20. ພູເອເວີເຣດ ສູງທີ່ສຸດໃນໂລກ. — Mount Everest is the highest mountain in the world.

T 69 Classroom ຫ້ອງຮຽນ

1. ຄູ ກັບ ນັກຮຽນ ໄປໂຮງຮຽນ. — The teacher and the students go to school.
2. ໂຮງຮຽນຢູ່ໃກ້ກັບວັດ. — The school is near the temple.
3. ອາຈານສອນຫັງສີຢູ່ຫ້ອງຮຽນ. — The teacher teaches in the classroom.
4. ນັກຮຽນ ຮຽນຢູ່ໃນຫ້ອງຮຽນ. — The students study in the classroom.
5. ໃນຫ້ອງຮຽນມີໂຕະ ໕ ໜ່ວຍ ກັບຕັ່ງ ໕ ໜ່ວຍ — In the classroom there are 5 tables and 5 chairs.
6. ອາຈານຂຽນຫັງສີໃສ່ກະດານ. — The teacher writes on the board.
7. ນັກຮຽນ ຂຽນຫັງສີໃສ່ປຶ້ມຂຽນ. — The students write in a notebook.
8. ນັກຮຽນທັງໝົດ ອ່ານ ບົດຫັດອ່ານ. — All of the students read the reading practice unit.
9. ແມ່ນຫຍັງ ຢູ່ເທິງໂຕະ? — What is on the table?
10. ປຶ້ມອ່ານ, ປຶ້ມຂຽນ ແລະບິກ ຢູ່ເທິງໂຕະ. — The book, notebook and pen are on the table.
11. ສໍດຳຢູ່ໃສ? — Where is the pencil?

Shapes and Sounds

12. ສໍດິຢູ່ກ້ອງຕັ່ງ. — The pencil is under the chair.
13. ນັກຮຽນມີບິກແດງບໍ? — Do the students have red pens?
14. ບໍ່ມີ, ພວກເຮົາມີບິກສີຟ້າ. — No, we don't. We have blue pens.
15. ອາຈານເວົ້າ. ນັກຮຽນຟັງ. — The teacher speaks. The students listen.
16. ອາຈານເວົ້າພາສາລາວ. ນັກຮຽນອ່ານພາສາລາວ. — The teacher speaks Lao. The students read Lao.
17. ນັກຮຽນເວົ້າພາສາອັງກິດ, ອາຈານຟັງບໍ່ເຂົ້າໃຈ. — The students speak English; the teacher doesn't understand.
18. ເຂົ້າໃຈບໍ? — Do you understand?
19. ເວລາອາຈານອະທິບາຍເປັນ ພາສາລາວ, ນັກຮຽນບໍ່ເຂົ້າໃຈ ປານໃດ. — When the teacher explains in Lao, the students do not understand very well.
20. ເວລາອາຈານອະທິບາຍເປັນ ພາສາອັງກິດ, ນັກຮຽນ ເຂົ້າໃຈດີ. — When the teacher explains in English, the students understand well.

T 70 Can You Speak Lao? ເວົ້າພາສາລາວໄດ້ບໍ?

1. ເຈົ້າເວົ້າພາສາລາວໄດ້ບໍ? — Can you speak Lao?
2. ຂ້ອຍເວົ້າພາສາລາວໄດ້ໜ້ອຍໜຶ່ງ. — I can speak Lao a little.
3. ເຈົ້າອ່ານພາສາລາວໄດ້ບໍ? — Can you read Lao?

4. ພວກເຮົາອ່ານກັບຂຽນພາສາລາວໄດ້. — We all can read and write Lao.
5. ເຈົ້າຮຽນຢູ່ໃສ? — Where do you study?
6. ຮຽນຢູ່ເມືອງນິວຢອກ, ປະເທດອາເມລິກາ. — I study in New York City, America.
7. ຮຽນພາສາລາວມ່ວນບໍ? — Do you enjoy learning Lao?
8. ມ່ວນ, ແຕ່ເມື່ອຍຫຼາຍ. — Yes, I do enjoy it. But (I get) very tired.
9. ພາສາລາວຍາກບໍ? — Is Lao difficult?
10. ຍາກ, ແຕ່ພາສາຈີນຍາກກວ່າ ພາສາລາວຫຼາຍ. — Yes, it is difficult. But Chinese is a lot more difficult than Lao.
11. ພາສາອັງກິດງ່າຍແມ່ນບໍ? — English is easy, right?
12. ແມ່ນແລ້ວ, ພາສາອັງກິດງ່າຍທີ່ສຸດ. — Definitely. English is the easiest.
13. ຢູ່ປະເທດລາວສະບາຍບໍ? — Is it comfortable living in Laos?
14. ສະບາຍດີ ແຕ່ຮ້ອນໜ້ອຍໜຶ່ງ. — Yes, it is. But it is a little hot.
15. ເຈົ້າກິນອາຫານເຜັດໄດ້ບໍ? — Can you eat spicy food?
16. ໄດ້, ຖ້າບໍ່ເຜັດຫຼາຍ. — Yes, I can, if it is not very spicy.
17. ເຈົ້າມັກຫຍັງຫຼາຍທີ່ສຸດ. — What do you like the most?
18. ຂ້ອຍມັກປະເທດລາວຫຼາຍທີ່ສຸດ. — I like Laos the most.

19. ເຈົ້າເວົ້າພາສາລາວເກັ່ງ ຫຼາຍ. — You speak Lao very well.
20. ບໍ່ເກັ່ງດອກ, ເວົ້າໄດ້ ໜ້ອຍ ດຽວເທົ່ານັ້ນ. — Not that well, really. I can just speak a little.

T 71 What Day is Today? ມື້ນີ້ແມ່ນວັນຫຍັງ?

1. ມື້ນີ້ແມ່ນວັນຫຍັງ? — What day is today?
2. ມື້ນີ້ແມ່ນວັນຈັນ. — Today is Monday.
3. ມື້ອື່ນແມ່ນວັນຫຍັງ? — What day is tomorrow?
4. ມື້ອື່ນແມ່ນວັນອັງຄານ. — Tomorrow is Tuesday.
5. ວັນອັງຄານ ແລ້ວແມ່ນວັນຫຍັງ? — What day is the day after Tuesday?
6. ວັນອັງຄານ ແລ້ວແມ່ນວັນພຸດ. — The day after Tuesday is Wednesday.
7. ມື້ວານນີ້ແມ່ນວັນອາທິດ ແມ່ນບໍ? — Yesterday was Sunday, wasn't it?
8. ແມ່ນແລ້ວ. — Yes, it was.
9. ພວກເຮົາຮຽນພາສາລາວ ທຸກມື້ ນອກຈາກວັນ ອາທິດ. — We study Lao every day except Sunday.
10. ພວກເຮົາແລ່ນຕອນເຊົ້າ ທຸກມື້ ນອກຈາກວັນ ອາທິດ. — We jog every morning except Sunday.
11. ວັນຈັນຢູ່ຕິດກັບວັນ ອັງຄານ. — Monday is next to Tuesday.

Shapes and Sounds

12.	ວັນອັງຄານຢູ່ລະຫວ່າງ ວັນຈັນ ກັບວັນພຸດ.	Tuesday is in between Monday and Wednesday.
13.	ນັກຮຽນມັກວັນອາທິດ ຫຼາຍທີ່ສຸດ.	The students like Sunday the most.
14.	ເປັນຫຍັງນັກຮຽນຈິ່ງມັກ ວັນອາທິດ?	Why do the students like Sunday?
15.	ເພາະວ່າວັນອາທິດແມ່ນ ມື້ພັກ.	Because Sunday is a day off.
16.	ວັນອາທິດນີ້ ເຈົ້າຊິໄປ ໃສ?	Where are you going to go this Sunday?
17.	ວັນອາທິດນີ້ຂ້ອຍຊິໄປ ໃນເມືອງ.	This Sunday I am going to go downtown.
18.	ເຈົ້າຊິໄປໃນເມືອງເຮັດ ຫຍັງ?	What are you going to do downtown?
19.	ຂ້ອຍຊິໄປຢາມໝູ່ຢູ່ ບໍລິສັດລົດເມ.	I am going to visit my friend at the bus company.
20.	ຕອນບ່າຍມື້ນີ້ ຂ້ອຍຊິໄປ ຕີບານກັບນັກສຶກສາລາວ.	This afternoon I am going to play volleyball with Lao students.

T 72 Day Month Year ວັນ ເດືອນ ປີ

1.	ຫົກສິບວິນາທີ ເທົ່າ ກັບໜຶ່ງ ນາທີ.	Sixty seconds equals one minute.
2.	ຫົກສິບນາທີ ເທົ່າກັບໜຶ່ງ ຊົ່ວໂມງ.	Sixty minutes equals one hour.
3.	ຊາວສີ່ຊົ່ວໂມງເທົ່າ ກັບໜຶ່ງມື້.	Twenty-four hours equals one day.
4.	ໜຶ່ງມື້ມີຈັກຊົ່ວໂມງ?	How many hours are there in one day?

Shapes and Sounds

5. ມື້ງນຶ່ງມີຊາວສີ່ຊົ່ວໂມງ. — One day has twenty-four hours.
6. ອາທິດນຶ່ງມີເຈັດວັນ. — One week has seven days.
7. ເຈັດມື້ເທົ່າກັບນຶ່ງອາທິດ. — Seven days equals one week.
8. ນຶ່ງເດືອນມີປະມານ ສີ່ອາທິດ. — One month has about four weeks.
9. ເດືອນນຶ່ງມີປະມານສາມສິບ ຫຼືສາມສິບເອັດມື້. — One month has about thirty or thirty-one days.
10. ເດືອນນີ້ ມີຈັກມື້? — How many days does this month have?
11. ເດືອນນີ້ແມ່ນເດືອນເມສາ ມີສາມສິບມື້. — This month is April; it has thirty days.
12. ເດືອນໜ້າເດ? — How about next month?
13. ເດືອນພຶດສະພາ ມີສາມສິບເອັດມື້. — May has thirty-one days.
14. ນຶ່ງປີ ມີສາມຮ້ອຍຫົກສິບຫ້າມື້ ແມ່ນບໍ? — One year has three hundred sixty-five days, doesn't it?
15. ແມ່ນແລ້ວ ສາມຮ້ອຍຫົກສິບຫ້າມື້ ຫຼືສິບສອງເດືອນ. — Yes, it does—three hundred sixty-five days or twelve months.
16. ເຈົ້າມາຮອດວຽງຈັນມື້ໃດ? — When did you arrive in Vientiane?
17. ພວກເຮົາມາຮອດວຽງຈັນ ທ່າງສາມອາທິດກ່ອນ. — We arrived in Vientiane about three weeks ago.
18. ພວກເຮົາເລີ່ມຮຽນພາສາລາວ ທ່າງສອງອາທິດກ່ອນ. — We started to study Lao about two weeks ago.

19. ພວກເຮົາພົບຄົນລາວ   We met Lao people about
    ທ່າງໆ ເດືອນກ່ອນ.   one month ago.
20. ສອງເດືອນກ່ອນ ພວກ   We met each other in
    ເຮົາ ພົບກັນຢູ່ກຸງເທບ.   Bangkok two months ago.

T 73   This Year—Last Year   ປີນີ້-ປີກາຍ

1. ປີນີ້ແມ່ນປີ ໒໐໐໒.   This year is 2002.
2. ປີກາຍແມ່ນປີ ໒໐໐໑.   Last year was 2001.
3. ປີໜ້າແມ່ນປີ ໒໐໐໓.   Next year is 2003.
4. ປີນີ້ວັນຊາດລາວຄົບຮອບ ຊາວເຈັດປີ.   This year is the twenty-seventh anniversary of the Lao National Day.
5. ເຈົ້າອາຍຸຈັກປີ?   How old are you?
6. ຂ້ອຍ ອາຍຸຊາວຫົກປີ.   I am twenty-six years old.
7. ເຈົ້າຊິໄປແຂວງຫຼວງພະບາງມື້ໃດ?   When are you going to go to Luang Prabang province?
8. ອີກສອງອາທິດ.   In two more weeks.
9. ອີກສາມອາທິດ ພວກເຮົາ ຊິເລີ່ມຕົ້ນເຮັດວຽກ.   In three more weeks we are going to start working.
10. ເຈົ້າຈະເຮັດວຽກຢູ່ລາວຈັກປີ?   How many years will you work in Laos.
11. ປະມານສອງປີ.   About two years.
12. ອີກສອງປີພວກເຮົາຈະເມືອ ປະເທດອາເມຣິກາ.   In about two years we are going to go back to America.
13. ປີກາຍເຈົ້າຢູ່ໃສ?   Where were you last year?

14. ປີກາຍຂ້ອຍຮຽນຢູ່ ມະຫາວິທະຍາໄລ ຊິກາ ໂກ. — Last year I studied at the University of Chicago.

15. ສອງປີກ່ອນຂ້ອຍເຮັດ ວຽກ ຢູ່ບໍລິສັດ ເປັບຊິ. — For the last two years I worked at Pepsi (company).

16. ວັນເສົາແລ້ວ ພວກ ເຮົາໄປ ທ່ຽວສວນ ວັດທະນະທຳ. — Last Saturday we went touring to the Cultural park.

17. ວັນເສົາໜ້າ ຂ້ອຍຈະ ສອນ ພາສາອັງກິດ ໃຫ້ອາຈານ. — Next Saturday I am going to teach English to the professor.

18. ຕອນແລງວັນເສົາ ພວກ ເຮົາ ໄປທ່ຽວໃນເມືອງ. — Saturday evening we are going touring downtown.

19. ຕອນແລງວັນເສົາ ກັບ ວັນອາທິດ ພວກ ເຮົາເບິ່ງໜັງ. — Saturday and Sunday evenings we watch movies.

20. ພວກເຮົາມັກໄປເບິ່ງໜັງ ນຳກັບຫຼາຍໆຄົນ. — We like to go watch movies together with a lot of people.

T 74 What Time is It? ຈັກໂມງແລ້ວ?

1. ຈັກໂມງແລ້ວ? — What time is it?
2. ເຈັດໂມງເຄິ່ງແລ້ວ. — It is half past seven.
3. ເຈົ້າເລີ່ມຮຽນຈັກໂມງ? — What time do you start to study?
4. ແປດໂມງ. — Eight o'clock.
5. ຢູ່ລາວ ໂຮງຮຽນເຂົ້າຈັກ ໂມງ? — What time do the schools in Laos start?

6.	ຕາມທຳມະດາແປດໂມງ.	Usually at eight o'clock.
7.	ໂຮງຮຽນເລີກຈັກໂມງ?	What time do the schools finish?
8.	ສີ່ໂມງ ຫຼືສີ່ໂມງເຄິ່ງ.	Four o'clock or half past four.
9.	ເຈົ້າເຂົ້າການຈັກໂມງ?	What time do you start work?
10.	ແປດໂມງ.	At eight o'clock.
11.	ເຈົ້າອອກຈາກເຮືອນຈັກ ໂມງ?	What time do you leave home?
12.	ຂ້ອຍອອກຈາກເຮືອນ ປະມານເຈັດໂມງເຄິ່ງ.	I leave home about half past seven.
13.	ເຈົ້າໄປເຖິງຫ້ອງການ ເວລາ ຈັກໂມງ?	What time do you arrive at the office?
14.	ຂ້ອຍໄປເຖິງກ່ອນແປດ ໂມງ.	I arrive before eight o'clock.
15.	ເຈົ້າຮູ້ບໍ ວ່າລົດເມໄປຂົວ ມິດຕະພາບ ອອກເວລາ ຈັກໂມງ?	Do you know what time the bus to the Friendship Bridge leaves?
16.	ເຈັດໂມງກົງ.	At seven o'clock sharp.
17.	ລົດເມໄປຮອດຂົວ ປະມານ ເຈັດໂມງເຄິ່ງ.	The bus arrives at the bridge at about half past seven.
18.	ລົດເມກັບມາຕະຫຼາດເຊົ້າ ປະມານ ໘ ໂມງ ໑໕.	The bus returns to the morning market at about 8:15.
19.	ຢູ່ນີ້ ພວກເຮົາ ກິນເຂົ້າທ່ຽງ ສິບ ເອັດໂມງປາຍ.	Here we eat lunch a little after eleven o'clock.

Shapes and Sounds

20. ຕອນບ່າຍ ພວກເຮົາເລີ່ມ ຮຽນບ່າຍໂມງກົງ. In the afternoon we start to study at one o'clock sharp.

T 75 Family ຄອບຄົວ

1. ຄອບຄົວຂອງເຈົ້າສະບາຍດີບໍ? — How is your family?
2. ສະບາຍດີ. ຂອບໃຈ. — Fine. Thank you.
3. ຄອບຄົວຂອງເຈົ້າຢູ່ໃສ? — Where does your family live?
4. ພໍ່ແມ່ຂອງຂ້ອຍຢູ່ເມືອງແອັດແລນຕ້າ. — My parents live in Atlanta.
5. ເຈົ້າມີອ້າຍເອື້ອຍນ້ອງຈັກຄົນ? — How many brothers and sisters do you have?
6. ສາມຄົນ. ຂ້ອຍເປັນລູກຜູ້ທີ່ສອງ. — Three. I am the second child.
7. ອ້າຍແລະນ້ອງຂອງເຈົ້າຢູ່ກັບພໍ່ແມ່ບໍ? — Do your brothers and sisters live with your parents?
8. ບໍ່ແມ່ນ. ອ້າຍຢູ່ເມືອງ ວໍຊິງຕັນ. — No. My older brother lives in Washington D.C.
9. ອ້າຍຂອງເຈົ້າສ້າງຄອບຄົວ ແລ້ວບໍ? — Is your brother married already?
10. ສ້າງຄອບຄົວແລ້ວ. ລາວມີລູກສອງຄົນ. — Yes, he is already married. He has two children.
11. ລູກສາວ ຫຼືລູກຊາຍ? — Daughters or sons?
12. ລູກສາວທັງສອງຄົນ. — Both are daughters.
13. ເຈົ້າມີນ້ອງສາວ ຫຼືນ້ອງຊາຍ? — Do you have a younger brother or sister?

14. ຂ້ອຍມີນ້ອງຊາຍ. ຂ້ອຍເປັນ ລູກສາວຜູ້ດຽວ. — I have a younger brother. I am the only daughter.
15. ພໍ່ແມ່ຮັກຂ້ອຍຫຼາຍ. — My parents love me very much.
16. ເຈົ້າຄິດຮອດພໍ່ແມ່ບໍ? — Do you miss your parents?
17. ຄິດຮອດຫຼາຍ. — I miss them a lot.
18. ດຽວນີ້ ນ້ອງຊາຍຂ້ອຍຢູ່ນຳພໍ່ແມ່. — Right now my younger brother lives with my parents.
19. ນ້ອງຊາຍຂອງເຈົ້າເຮັດວຽກຫຍັງ? — Where does your younger brother work?
20. ລາວກຳລັງຮຽນຢູ່ມະຫາວິທະຍາໄລ. — He is studying at the university.

T 76 Luang Prabang ເມືອງຫຼວງພະບາງ (Lōuang Pha'bāng)

1. ເມືອງຫຼວງພະບາງເປັນເມືອງນ້ອຍ ແຕ່ງາມຫຼາຍ. — Luang Prabang is a small city but very beautiful.
2. ຫຼວງພະບາງແມ່ນເມືອງມໍລະດົກໂລກ. — Luang Prabang is a World Heritage city.
3. ເມືອງນີ້ມີສະຖານທີ່ທ່ອງທ່ຽວຫຼາຍແຫ່ງ. — The city has many tourist sites.
4. ສະຖານທີ່ທ່ອງທ່ຽວທີ່ສຳຄັນ ມີຫຍັງແດ່? — What important tourist sites are there?
5. ມີ ຫໍພິພິຕະພັນລາຊະວັງ, ວັດຊຽງທອງ, ຖ້ຳຕິ່ງແລະອື່ນໆ. — There is the royal Palace Museum, Sīeng Thọng temple, Tham Dting cave, and others.

Shapes and Sounds

6. ເມືອງຫຼວງພະບາງມີວັດ ແລະ ເຮືອນລາວ ແບບ ບູຮານ ຫຼາຍແທ້ໆ. — Luang Prabang has many temples and ancient-style houses.
7. ເມືອງຫຼວງພະບາງບໍ່ມີ ຮ້ານ ຊຸບພະສິນຄ້າ. — Luang Prabang doesn't have a supermarket.
8. ແຕ່ເມືອງຫຼວງພະບາງມີ ຕະຫຼາດຫຼາຍແທ້ໆ. — But Luang Prabang has many markets.
9. ຕະຫຼາດທີ່ໃຫຍ່ທີ່ສຸດແມ່ນ ຕະຫຼາດໂພສີ. — The biggest market is the Phōsī market.
10. ເມືອງນີ້ມີຮ້ານອາຫານບໍ? — Does the city have any restaurants?
11. ມີ, ມີຮ້ານອາຫານຫຼາຍ ແທ້ໆ. ຮ້ານອາຫານທີ່ມີ ຊື່ສຽງ ແມ່ນຮ້ານກາເຟ ແຊຟຣອນ. — Yes, it does. There are many restaurants. A popular restaurant is the Saffron coffee shop.
12. ຮ້ານອາຫານແຫ່ງນີ້ຕັ້ງຢູ່ ແຄມຂອງ. — This restaurant is located on the Mekong River.
13. ເວລາທີ່ເໝາະສົມສຳລັບ ໄປ ທ່ອງທ່ຽວຫຼວງພະ ບາງແມ່ນກາງເດືອນ ເມສາ. — A good time to visit Luang Prabang is in the middle of April.
14. ໃນຍາມນີ້ ມັກທ່ອງ ທ່ຽວຈະໄປທ່ຽວຫຼວງພະ ບາງຫຼາຍ. — At this time many tourists go to visit Luang Prabang.
15. ເມື່ອໄດ້ມາລາວແລ້ວ, ຖ້າບໍ່ເຫັນຫຼວງພະບາງ ກໍ ເທົ່າກັບຍັງບໍ່ທັນ ເຫັນ ເມືອງລາວເທື່ອ. — When you come to Laos, if you don't see Luang Prabang it is like you haven't seen Laos yet.

T 77 Lao New Year ປີໃໝ່ລາວ

1. ມື້ໃດ ຈະຮອດວັນປີໃໝ່ລາວ? — When is the Lao New Year?
2. ວັນທີ ໑໔ ເດືອນເມສາ. — The fourteenth of April.
3. ຄືກັນທຸກໆ ປີທ້ວາ? — Is it the same every year?
4. ເຈົ້າ ຄືກັນທຸກປີ. — Yes. It is the same every year.
5. ວັນປີໃໝ່ລາວເປັນວັນສຳຄັນ ຂອງຄົນລາວ. — Lao New Year is an important day for Lao people.
6. ວັນປີໃໝ່ລາວເປັນມື້ພັກທາງ ລັດຖະການ. — Lao New Year is an official holiday.
7. ໃນວັນປີໃໝ່ ຄົນລາວຈະເດີນທາງໄປຢ້ຽມຍາມພີ່ນ້ອງ. — During Lao New Year Lao people go to visit their relatives.
8. ຢູ່ຕາມເຮືອນຄົນລາວມັກຈະເຮັດພິທີບາສີສູ່ຂວັນ ເພື່ອຕ້ອນຮັບ ປີໃໝ່. — In Lao homes Lao people like to do the Bāsī Sōu Khwan ceremony to welcome the new year.
9. ນັກທ່ອງທ່ຽວຕ່າງປະເທດ ມັກ ເດີນທາງໄປ ຫຼວງພະບາງ ໃນຍາມບຸນປີໃໝ່. — Foreign tourists like to go to Luang Prabang during the Lao New Year holiday.
10. ໃນຍາມ ບຸນປີໃໝ່, ຢູ່ຫຼວງພະບາງ ມີພິທີແຫ່ນາງ ສັງຂານ. — During the Lao New Year holiday in Luang Prabang there is the Miss Sangkhān Parade.
11. ປີໃໝ່ລາວ ຢູ່ແຕ່ລະແຂວງ ມ່ວນຫຼາຍ. ແຕ່ຢູ່ຫຼວງພະບາງມ່ວນກວ່າໝູ່. — Lao New Year in each province is very fun. But in Luang Prabang it is the most fun.

Shapes and Sounds

12. ຜູ້ບ່າວຜູ້ສາວ ມັກໄປສົງ ພະຢູ່ວັດ.
    Guys and girls like to pour water on the Buddha image at the temple.

13. ບາງຄົນໄປຫົດ ນໍ້າອວຍພອນ ໃຫ້ແກ່ຜູ້ ທີ່ຕົນນັບຖື.
    Some people go to throw water on those they respect as a blessing.

14. ເຈົ້າອາດຈະຖືກຫົດ ນໍ້າ ເວລາເຈົ້າຍ່າງ ໄປຕາມຖະໜົນ.
    You might get water thrown on you when you walk along the street.

15. ເຈົ້າອາດຈະຄຽດ ຖ້າ ເຈົ້າບໍ່ ເຂົ້າໃຈປະເພນີ ລາວ.
    You might get angry if you don't understand the Lao custom.

T 78 Vientiane (Vīang Chan) ວຽງຈັນ

1. ວຽງຈັນເປັນເມືອງ ຫຼວງຂອງ ສ.ປ.ປ. ລາວ.
   Vientiane is the capital city of the Lao P.D.R.

2. ວໍຊິງຕັນເປັນ ນະຄອນຫຼວງຂອງ ປະ ເທດ ສະຫະລັດ ອາ ເມຣິກາ.
   Washington is the capital city of The United States of America.

3. ທັງວຽງຈັນແລະວໍຊິງຕັນ ເປັນເມືອງສຳຄັນ.
   Both Vientiane and Washington are important cities.

4. ສະຖານທີ່ສຳຄັນ ຕ່າງໆ ຢູ່ ວຽງຈັນມີ ກະຊວງ,ສະຖານທູດ, ວັດ, ໂຮງຮຽນ ແລະ ອື່ນໆ.
   The important places in Vientiane are government ministries, embassies, temples, schools and others.

Shapes and Sounds

5. ເຈົ້າໄຂຍະເສດຖາທິລາດ ໄດ້ນຳພາ ປະຊາຊົນສ້າງ ນະຄອນຫຼວງວຽງຈັນ.
King Sainya Sēthāthilāt led the people to build the capital Vientiane.

6. ພະທາດຫຼວງແລະຫໍພະ ແກ້ວ ຖືກສ້າງຂຶ້ນ ໃນສະ ໄໝຂອງ ເຈົ້າໄຂຍະເສດ ຖາທິລາດ.
That Luang Stupa and Hō Pha'Gkāeo Temple were built in the time of King Sainya' Sēthāthilāt.

7. ວັດສີສະເກດຖືກສ້າງ ຂຶ້ນໃນ ສະໄໝຂອງ ເຈົ້າອານຸວົງ.
Sisaket Temple was built in the time of King Ānou' Vong.

8. ປັດຈຸບັນນີ້ ມີຄົນຢູ່ ໃນວຽງຈັນ ເກືອບຮອດຫ້າແສນຄົນ.
Presently there are almost five hundred thousand people in Vientiane.

9. ຖະໜົນສາຍສຳຄັນຢູ່ ວຽງຈັນມີ ຖະໜົນລ້ານ ຊ້າງ, ຖະໜົນ ສາມແສນ ໄທ ແລະຖະໜົນ ເສດ ຖາທິລາດ.
Important streets in Vientiane are Lān Sāng Avenue, Sāmsāenthai Avenue and Sēthāthilāt Avenue.

10. ອາກາດຢູ່ວຽງຈັນຮ້ອນ ຫຼາຍໃນເດືອນເມສາ ແລະເດືອນ ພຶດສະພາ.
The weather in Vientiane is very hot during the months of April and May.

11. ຖະໜົນຕ່າງໆໃນວຽງຈັນ ມີລົດເມແລ່ນຮັບໃຊ້ ປະຊາຊົນຕະຫຼອດມື້.
Various streets in Vientiane have buses that serve the people all day long.

12. ເຈົ້າຕ້ອງຂຶ້ນ ແລະລົງລົດ ເມ ຢູ່ປ້າຍ.
You need to get on and off the bus at the bus stop.

13. ເວລາຂ້າມທາງຢູ່ສີ່ແຍກ ເຈົ້າຕ້ອງ ຂ້າມຢູ່ທາງມ້າ ລາຍ.
When you cross the intersection you need to cross at the crosswalk.

14. ໃບມົກຳມະດາຢູ່ຖະໜົນລ້ານຊ້າງມີລົດຕິດໃນໂມງເຂົ້າການແລະເລີກການ.

On a normal day on Lān Sāng Avenue there is a traffic jam at the time when work begins and finishes.

15. ເວລາເຈົ້າຊິໄປຕະຫຼາດເຂົ້າເຈົ້າຂຶ້ນລົດເມຢູ່ຂ້າງອ່າງນ້ຳ ດົງໂດກກໍໄດ້.

When you go to the market you can get the bus next to Dong Dok water tower.

7.7 Short Stories

Tracks 79-92 below are short stories in Lao.[1] Each of them have English translations below for the reader to refer to if help in understanding is needed. Listen to these stories in the audio. Try to get a feel for the rhythm and tones and how they are pronounced in normal speech. As you progress in your ability to read Lao, read these stories out loud along with the audio.

T 79 The Two Frogs ກົບສອງໂຕ

ຄັ້ງໜຶ່ງ ກົບສອງໂຕຕົກລົງໃນໄຫນ້ຳນົມ. ພວກມັນອອກຈາກໄຫບໍ່ໄດ້. ດັ່ງນັ້ນພວກມັນຈຶ່ງລອຍອ້ອມໄປອ້ອມມາຢູ່ໃນນ້ຳນົມ ກົບໂຕໜຶ່ງເລີຍເວົ້າວ່າ, "ໂອ, ນີ້ແມ່ນຂັ້ນສິ້ນສຸດຊີວິດຂອງກູແລ້ວເດ". ມັນເຊົາ ລອຍແລ້ວກໍຕາຍ. ແຕ່ວ່າກົບໂຕທີສອງກໍລອຍໄປລອຍມາແລ້ວກໍເອົາຕີນນ້ອຍໆ ຂອງຕົນຕົບນ້ຳນົມ. ນິມຂຸ້ນເຂົ້າແລ້ວກໍເລີຍ

---

[1] With the exception of "Living With Each Other" and "The Lost Son", all of these stories were taken from "Tales for Readers: English-Lao" written by Soukhine Manosone. Some of the translations have been reworked for better understanding. The story "Living With Each Other" is taken from the Lao publication written by Khamphāi Sisavan, and published by the Ministry of Education in Vientiane, Lao P.D.R., 1997. The English translation for "Living With Each Other" is new with this text. The story "The Lost Son" is taken from the Bible in the Lao Common Language published in 2000 by the UBS. The English translation for "The Lost Son" is new with this text.

ກາຍເປັນກ້ອນເນີຍ. ກົບໂຕນັ້ນກໍເຕັ້ນຂຶ້ນໜ່ອຍເນີຍ ແລ້ວ ກໍອອກຈາກໄຫໄປໄດ້.

Once two frogs fell into a pot of milk. They could not get out of the pot. So they swam around and around in the milk. Said one of them, "Oh, this is the end of my life." It stopped swimming and died.

But the second frog swam and swam and beat the milk with its little feet. The milk became a ball of butter. The frog jumped on the ball of butter and got out of the pot!

T 80 Living With Each Other ການຢູ່ໃສກັນ

ຕອນສວາຍມື້ໜຶ່ງ ແດດຮ້ອນ... ຮ້ອນ... ໄກ່ແມ່ຟັກທົວບຳຈຶ່ງ ໂຕນຈາກຮັງຮ້ອງ, "ກຸ໊ກ! ກຸ໊ກ! ກຸ໊ກ!" ແລ່ນໄປກິນນຳ ຢູ່ຮົ່ມຕົ້ນມ່ວງ.

ໄກ່ຜູ້ໂອກງອຍຮື້ວຕົບປີກ "ປຶບ! ປຶບ! ປຶບ!" ແລ້ວກໍ່ງຳຂັນ: "ເອິກອິເອິເອິກ..." ຈາກນັ້ນມັນໂຕນຮື້ວ ແລ່ນໄປໃສ່ໄກ່ແມ່ຟັກ.

ໄກ່ແມ່ຟັກເວົ້າກັບໄກ່ຜູ້ໂອກວ່າ, "ເຈົ້າຫັ້ນກິນອິ່ມແລ້ວ ມີແຕ່ທ່ຽວຫລິ້ນ, ເບິ່ງຂ້ອຍແມ ຟັກໄຂ່ທັງເວັນທັງຄືນ ເຂົ້ານຳກໍກິນບໍ່ອິ່ມ, ບໍ່ຄືນຊິໄດ້ລ້ຽງລູກອີກ."

ໄກ່ຜູ້ໂອກຕອບວ່າ: "ເຈົ້າທະດາຍມັກຕິແຕ່ໝູ່ບໍ. ຂ້ອຍ ກໍຂັນບອກເວລາເປັນໄລຍະທັງເວັນທັງຄືນທັ້ນເດ. ຂ້ອຍຊິ ແຈ້ງຍິ່ງຂັນດຸເພື່ອປຸກຄົນລຸກໄປເຮັດວຽກ."

ຕອນເດິກຂອງຄືນນັ້ນໄກ່ແມ່ຟັກອົບທັບມີງູສາໂຕ ໜຶ່ງເລື້ອເຂົ້າມາໃກ້ຮັງພໍດີກັບເວລາໄກ່ຜູ້ໂອກຕົບປີກຂັນ.

ໄກ່ແມ່ຟັກຕິ່ນສງຸງຂັນມືນຕາຂຶ້ນເຫັນງູສາໂຕບັກໃຫຍ່ ແລບລີ້ນຢູ່ໃກ້ໆ ຕົນເອງ. ຈິ່ງຮ້ອງຂຶ້ນວ່າ: "ຂ້ອຍແດ່! ຂ້ອຍແດ່!"

ໄກ່ຜູ້ໂອກໄດ້ຍິນກຳຟັງວມາຂ້ອຍແລ້ວໂດດເຕະຄຳງ
ໜົດແຮງໆ. ງູອ້າປາກຈະຕອດໄກ່ແຕ່ໄກ່ສັບທີວງໆ ແລະ
ເຕະກ້ານຄຳກ່ອນ ສອງ-ສາມ ບາດ.
ງູເຈັບສູ້ບໍ່ໄທວຈິ່ງເລືອໜີໄປ.
ໄກ່ແມ່: "ອ້າຍໂອກເອີຍ ຂອບໃຈຫລາຍໆເນີ,
ຖ້າເຈົ້າບໍ່ຊ່ອຍ ຂ້ອຍຄົງຈະຕາຍແລ້ວ."
ໄກ່ຜູ້: "ບໍ່ເປັນຫຍັງດອກ ເຮົາຕ້ອງຊ່ອຍເຫຼືອກັນ."

Late one morning the sun was hot… hot… The mother hen was thirsty. So she jumped from her nest, crying, "Gouk! Gouk! Gouk!" and she ran to drink some water in the shade of a mango tree.

The big rooster perched on the fence and flapped his wings, "Pewp! Pewp! Pewp!" Then he arched his neck and crowed, "Uuk-i-uuk-uuk!" After that he jumped off the fence and ran to the mother hen.

The mother hen spoke with the rooster, saying, "Hey you there! You eat your fill and then all you do is play. Look at me! I sit on my eggs all day and all night. I don't eat enough food and water. Before long I will have children to feed, too."

The big rooster answered, saying, "You here—you only like to criticize others. I crow to indicate the time period all of these days and nights. When it is almost daylight I crow loud and often in order to wake the people up to go to work."

That night when it was dark and the mother hen was sleeping well, a Saa snake slithered inside near the nest. At just that time the big rooster flapped his wings and crowed. The mother hen awoke at the sound of the crow and opened her eyes. She saw the big Saa snake sticking his tongue in and out very near to her. So she cried out, saying "Help! Help!"

The big rooster heard and quickly came to help. Then he jumped on and kicked the snake's neck with all his strength. The snake opened his mouth to strike the chicken, but the chicken pecked the snake's head first and kicked the back of his neck two or three times. The snake was hurt. He was not able to fight successfully so he slithered away.

The mother hen said, "Dear brother rooster, thank you very much! If you had not helped I would already be dead!"
The rooster said, "It is really no problem. We should help one another."

T 81 The Story about the Tongue ນິທານເລື່ອງລິ້ນ

ຄັ້ງໜຶ່ງທ້າວໜ້າໄດ້ບອກໃຫ້ຄົນໃຊ້ຜູ້ໜຶ່ງໄປເອົາ ຊີ້ນຊະນິດດີທີ່ສຸດໃນຕະຫຼາດມາໃຫ້ເພິ່ນ. ຄົນໃຊ້ກໍໄດ້ເອົາລິ້ນມາໃຫ້ເພິ່ນ.

ມື້ຕໍ່ມາທ້າວໜ້າກໍໄດ້ບອກໃຫ້ ຄົນໃຊ້ຜູ້ນັ້ນໄປເອົາຊີ້ນ ຂີ້ຮ້າຍທີ່ສຸດໃນຕະຫຼາດມາໃຫ້ເພິ່ນ. ຄົນໃຊ້ກໍເອົາລິ້ນ ມາໃຫ້ເພິ່ນອິກ.

ທ້າວໜ້າເລີຍເວົ້າຂຶ້ນວ່າ "ແມ່ນຫຍັງບໍ? ເມື່ອກູຢາກໄດ້ ຊີ້ນດີທີ່ສຸດມຶງພັດເອົາລິ້ນມາໃຫ້ ແລະ ເມື່ອກູຢາກໄດ້ຊີ້ນ ຂີ້ຮ້າຍທີ່ສຸດມຶງຊ້ຳພັດເອົາລິ້ນຄືເກົ່າມາໃຫ້ກູ".

ຄົນໃຊ້ກໍເລີຍເວົ້າວ່າ: "ບາງເທື່ອຄົນບໍ່ມີຄວາມຜາສຸກ ໄດ້ກໍຍ້ອນລິ້ນຕົນເອງ ແລະ ບາງເທື່ອລິ້ນຕົນເອງເຮັດໃຫ້ມີ ຄວາມຜາສຸກໄດ້."

ທ້າວໜ້າເລີຍເວົ້າວ່າ: "ມຶງເວົ້າຖືກຕ້ອງ, ເອົາເທາະພວກ ເຮົາຈົ່ງນຳໃຊ້ລິ້ນຂອງພວກເຮົາໃຫ້ດີ!"

Once a chief told one of his servants to bring him the best meat from the market. The servant brought him a tongue

The next day the chief told the servant to bring him the worst meat from the market.

The servant brought him a tongue again.

The chief said, "What? When I ask for the best meat you bring a tongue and then you bring me the same thing for the worst meat."

The servant said, "Sometimes a man is very unhappy because of his tongue, and sometimes his tongue makes him very happy."

The chief said, "You are right. Let us be masters of our tongues!"

Shapes and Sounds

T 82 The Chicken at the Well ໄກ່ນ້ອຍຢູ່ບໍ້ສ້າງ

ແມ່ໄກ່ເວົ້າກັບລູກມັນວ່າ, "ຢ່າໄປໃກ້ບໍ້ສ້າງ ເດີພວກລູກເອີຍ! ພວກລູກທັງ ຫລາຍຢ່າແລ່ນຫລິ້ນຮ້ອມ ບໍ້ສ້າງເດີ!"

ລູກໄກ່ທັງຫລາຍກໍບໍ່ມາທາງບໍ້ສ້າງເລີຍ. ແຕ່ວ່າໃນດັ້ງ ນຶ່ງໄກ່ນ້ອຍໂຕນຶ່ງໄດ້ແລ່ນໄປທາງບໍ້ສ້າງແລ້ວຢຸດຢູ່ທີ່ ນັ້ນ.

ໄກ່ນ້ອຍຄິດວ່າ, "ເປັນຫຍັງບໍ້ສ້າງນີ້ມາຂີ້ຮ້າຍພິລຶກ ແທ້? ກູຢູ່ທີ່ນີ້ ແລະກໍບໍ່ເຫັນມີຫຍັງເກີດຂຶ້ນ. ກູຊິເບິ່ງ ກ່ອນວ່າແມ່ນຫຍັງຢູ່ບໍ້ສ້າງນີ້."

ມັນເຕັ້ນເຂົ້າໄປເບິ່ງບໍ້ສ້າງ. ມັນໄດ້ເຫັນຫຍັງ ແດ່ຢູ່ທັ້ນ? ມັນເຫັນໄກ່ນ້ອຍໂຕນຶ່ງອີກ! ໄກ່ນ້ອຍໂຕມັນ ງັ່ນຫົວຂອງມັນ, ໄກ່ນ້ອຍຢູ່ບໍ້ສ້າງກໍງັ່ນຫົວຕິກັນ. ໄກ່ນ້ອຍໂຕນີ້ເຕັ້ນ, ໄກ່ນ້ອຍ ໃນບໍ້ສ້າງກໍເຕັ້ນຕິກັນ. ມັນໃຈຮ້າຍໃຫ້ໄກ່ນ້ອຍຢູ່ບໍ້ສ້າງນັ້ນ ແລ້ວຕັດ ສິນໃຈຕິກັບມັນ, ມັນໂດດລົງໃນບໍ້ສ້າງ. ແຕ່ວ່າບໍ່ມີ ໄກ່ນ້ອຍຈັກໂຕເລີຍຕິກັບມັນ ມີແຕ່ນໍ້າເທົ່ານັ້ນ.

ມັນຮ້ອງໄຫ້, "ຊ່ອຍແດ່! ຊ່ອຍແດ່!" ແຕ່ບໍ່ມີໃຜໄດ້ ຍິນມັນເລີຍ. ມັນຈົມລົງພື້ນນໍ້າເຢັນ ແລະບໍ່ມີໃຜເຫັນ ມັນອີກເລີຍ.

The mother hen said to her children, "Don't go near the well! Don't play around it."

They never went to the well. But once a little chicken ran to the well and stopped there. He thought, "Why is the well so bad? I am here and everything is all right with me. Let me see what is in the well."

He jumped up to look into it. What did he see in there? He saw another chicken! The chicken turned his head, and the chicken in the

well did the same. The chicken jumped, and so did the chicken in
the well. He became angry with the chicken in the well and decided
to fight with him. He jumped down into the well. But there was no
chicken to fight with, only water.
He cried, "Help me! Help me!" But nobody heard him. He went
down under the cold water and nobody saw him again.

T 83 Why the Rabbit has no Tail
ເປັນຫຍັງກະຕ່າຍຈຶ່ງບໍ່ມີຫາງ

ດົນນານຜ່ານມາແລ້ວ ສັດທັງຫລາຍບໍ່ມີຫາງເລີຍ
ທລີ ມີກໍານ້ອຍທີ່ສຸດ. ມື້ນຶ່ງສິງໂຕນຶ່ງໄດ້ຮຽກຮ້ອງໃຫ້ສັດ
ທັງຫລາຍມາຫາເພື່ອຮັບເອົາຫາງທີ່ດີ. ໃນມື້ນັ້ນ
ອາກາດໜາວ ແລະຝົນຕົກ, ກະຕ່າຍ
ໂຕນຶ່ງມີພຽງແຕ່ຫາງນ້ອຍໆສັ້ນໆເທົ່ານັ້ນ,
ແຕ່ມັນບໍ່ຢາກອອກໄປນອກ ແລ້ວເວົ້າຕໍ່ສັດອື່ນໆວ່າ,
"ກະລຸນາເອົາຫາງມາໃຫ້ຂ້ອຍແດ່ເບີ. ຂ້ອຍ ໄປບໍ່ອນ
ອື່ນບໍ່ໄດ້ໃນເມື່ອ ຝົນຕົກ."

ສັດທັງຫລາຍຖາມມັນຄືນວ່າ, "ຫາງແບບໃດທີ່
ເຈົ້າຢາກໄດ້." "ໂອ, ຫາງແບບໃດກໍໄດ້ ວ່າແຕ່ມັນ
ເໝາະສົມກັບຂ້ອຍ. ແຕ່ຢ່າໃຫ້ມັນຍາວໂພດ ແລະ
ສັ້ນໂພດເດີ."

ພາຍຫລັງທີ່ສັດທັງຫລາຍໄດ້ກັບມາ, ສັດທຸກໂຕກໍໄດ້
ຫາງທີ່ສວຍງາມມາພ້ອມ. ແຕ່ບໍ່ມີໂຕໃດເອົາຫາງມາໃຫ້
ກະຕ່າຍເລີຍ.

ຂ້ອຍຄິດວ່າສັດຈໍານວນນຶ່ງລືມກະຕ່າຍເສຍແລ້ວ,
ຈໍານວນນຶ່ງກໍບໍ່ມີເວລາ ເລີຍ, ຈໍານວນນຶ່ງກໍບໍ່ສາມາດ
ຂອງຫາງດີໆໃຫ້ກະຕ່າຍໄດ້.

ແຕ່ເລື່ອງນີ້ຂ້ອຍກໍຮູ້ດີວ່າ: ຖ້າວ່າສິ່ງທີ່ທ່ານພຶ່ງເຮັດໄດ້ບໍ່

Shapes and Sounds

ຄວນຈະໃຊ້ຜູ້ອື່ນເຮັດໃຫ້. ຢ່າຊິລຶມແທ້ໆເດີເລື່ອງກະຕ່າຍ ກັບຫາງນ້ອຍສັ້ນໆຂອງມັນ!

Long, long ago the animals had no tails or they had very small ones. One day the lion asked all the animals to come to him to get good tails. It was cold that day and it was raining. The rabbit had only a short little tail, but he did not want to go out, so he said to the other animals, "Please bring me a tail. I can't go anywhere when it rains." The animals asked him, "What kind of tail do you want?"

"Oh, any tail will be good for me. But it must not be too long or too short."

Some time later the animals came back and each animal had a beautiful tail. But nobody brought a tail for the rabbit.

I think that some of them forgot about the rabbit; some had no time; some could not find a good tail for the rabbit.

But I know this: If you must do something, don't ask others to do it for you. Don't forget about the rabbit with his short little tail!

T 84 A Sly Cat ແມວຂີ້ຫລັກ

ເມື່ອມັນຍັງເປັນແມວໜຸ່ມທີ່ແຂງແຮງ, ມັນຄຸບໜູໄດ້ຕັ້ງຫລາຍໆໂຕ, ໜູທັງຫລາຍຢ້ານມັນ ແຕ່ໃນເວລາທີ່ມັນເຖົ້າແກ່ແລ້ວບໍ່ສາມາດຄຸບໜູໄດ້ອີກເລີຍ.

ມື້ໜຶ່ງມັນໄດ້ຕັດສິນໃຈທຳກົນອຸບາຍກັບໜູ. ມັນນອນຫງາຍ ແລະ ທຳບໍ່ເໜັງຕີງ ເລີຍ. ໜູໂຕໜຶ່ງເຫັນມັນ ແລະ ຄິດວ່າມັນຕາຍ. ໜູໂຕນັ້ນກໍເລີຍແລ່ນໄປຫາໝູ່ມັນແລ້ວເວົ້າວ່າ, "ແມວຕາຍແລ້ວເວີຍ! ພວກເຮົາມາເຕັ້ນລຳ ແລະ ແລ່ນຫລິ້ນກັນເທາະ!"

ໜູທຸກໂຕກໍພາກັນເຕັ້ນລຳ ແລະ ແລ່ນຫລິ້ນ. ພວກມັນສະໜຸກມ່ວນຊື່ນຫລາຍ. ພວກມັນ ເຕັ້ນລຳໄປເຕັ້ນລຳມາຮອບໂຕແມວ, ແມວກໍບໍ່ເໜັງຕີງເລີຍ. ບາດແລ້ວໜູ ໂຕໜຶ່ງເລີຍເຕັ້ນຂຶ້ນຂີ່ທິວແມວ ແລະ ເວົ້າວ່າ,

"ເບິ່ງກູແມ້ສູ! ພວກສູທັງໝົດທັບເຂົ້າມາໃກ້ໆກູແມ້!
ບັກແມວຂີ້ຂົ້ງໆນີ້ຕາຍແລ້ວເດ! ພວກເຮົາພາກັນມາເຕັ້ນ
ລຳຢູ່ເທິງຫົວມັນ ເທາະ!"
　　ທັນໃດນັ້ນ, ແມວໂຕນັ້ນກໍໂດດຄຸບເອົາໜູຂີ້ໂງ່ໂຕນັ້ນ.
ສ່ວນໜູໂຕອື່ນໆກໍແລ່ນ ໜີໄວບໍ່ຄ້ານ.
　　ໜູທັງຫລາຍເອີຍຢ່າລືມເດີ! ຢ່າຊິເຊື່ອບັກແມວຈັກ
ເທື່ອເລີຍ!

When he was a strong young cat he caught many mice. The mice were afraid of him then. But in time he grew old and could not catch mice any more.

One day he decided to play a trick on the mice. He laid on his back and did not move at all. A mouse saw him and thought he was dead. She ran to her friends and said: "The cat is dead! Let us dance and play!"

And all the mice began to dance and play. They were happy. They danced and danced around the cat, and the cat did not move. Then one of the mice jumped on the cat's head.

"Look at me! Come nearer, all of you! The bad cat is dead! Let us dance on his head!"

But suddenly the cat jumped up and caught the silly mouse. The other mice ran away as quickly as they could.

Mice! Don't forget: Never believe a cat!

T 85   The Smart Dog   ໝາສະຫລາດ

　　ມີໜຶ່ງໝາເກົ່າໂຕອອກໄປລ່າເນື້ອ.
ພວກມັນພົບເຫັນສິງໂຕໜຶ່ງ. ສິງໂຕນັ້ນ ເລີຍເວົ້າວ່າ,
"ຂ້ອຍພວມໄປລ່າເນື້ອຄືກັນ. ຂ້ອຍທົດຫລາຍພວກເຮົາໄປ
ລ່າເນື້ອນຳກັນເທາະເວີຍ!" ດັ່ງນັ້ນໝາ ແລະ ສິງຈິ່ງໄປລ່າ
ເນື້ອນຳກັນໝົດມື້. ພວກມັນຄຸບເຍື່ອໄດ້ສິບໂຕ.
　　ບາດແລ້ວສິງກໍເລີຍເວົ້າວ່າ, "ພວກເຮົາຄວນແບ່ງ

Shapes and Sounds

ຂຶ້ນກັບດວງນີ້ເທາະເວີຍ."

ໝາໂຕໜຶ່ງເລີຍເວົ້າວ່າ, "ມັນເປັນຂອງງ່າຍໆ. ພວກເຮົາມີສິບໂຕແລ້ວ ແລະພວກເຮົາກໍໄດ້ເຍື່ອງສິບໂຕ, ຈັ່ງຊັ້ນພວກເຮົາຈະໄດ້ເຍື່ອງຜູ້ລະໂຕລະ."

ອ້າຍສິງກໍຮ້າຍຂຶ້ນໝົດແຮງ. ມັນກໍຕີໝາໂຕນັ້ນຢ່າງໜ້າສັງເວດ ແລະ ກໍເຮັດໃຫ້ໝາໂຕນັ້ນຕາບອດ.

ສ່ວນໝາໂຕອື່ນໆບໍ່ເວົ້າຫຍັງເລີຍ.

ແຕ່ກໍມີໝາໂຕໜຶ່ງເວົ້າຂຶ້ນມາວ່າ, "ອ້າຍຂອງພວກເຮົາຜິດພາດໄປແລ້ວ. ພວກເຮົາຄວນເອົາເຍື່ອງເກົ້າໂຕໃຫ້ພະຍາສິງສາ. ພວກເພິ່ນຈິ່ງຈະຄົບສິບພໍດີ. ແລ້ວພວກເຮົາກໍຈະເອົາເຍື່ອງໂຕໜຶ່ງ, ແລ້ວພວກເຮົາກໍຈະຄົບສິບຄືກັນ."

ອ້າຍສິງມັກຄຳຕອບຂອງໝາໂຕນັ້ນແລ້ວຖາມວ່າ, "ໃຜສອນໃຫ້ບິງແບ່ງປັນຄືແບວນີ້? ມິງເປັນໝາໂຕສະຫລາດນໍ".

ໝາໂຕນັ້ນກໍເລີຍຕອບວ່າ, "ໂອຍ, ພະຍາສິງເອີຍ, ທ່ານໄດ້ຕີອ້າຍຂອງພວກຂ້ານ້ອຍຈົນຕາລາວບອດ. ອ້າຍຜູ້ຕາບອດນັ້ນແລ້ວສອນຂ້ານ້ອຍພະຍາສິງເອີຍ!"

One day nine dogs went out to hunt. They met a lion. The lion said, "I am hunting, too. I am very, very hungry. Let us hunt together." So the dogs and the lion hunted together all day. They caught ten antelopes.

Then the lion said, "Now we must divide the meat."

One of the dogs said, "Why, that's easy. We are ten, and we have ten antelopes. So, each one of us will have one antelope."

The lion became very angry. He hit the poor dog and blinded him. The other dogs did not say a word. But then one of the dogs said, "Our brother was wrong. We must give nine antelopes to King Lion. Then they will be ten together. And we dogs shall take one antelope, and we shall also be ten together."

The lion liked his answer and asked the dog, "Who taught you to divide like this? You are a wise dog."

The dog answered, "Oh, King Lion! You hit our brother and blinded him. That brother taught me, King Lion!"

T 86 The Frog and his Wives ກົບ ແລະ ເມຍ ຂອງມັນ

ຄັ້ງໜຶ່ງຍັງມີກົບໂຕໜຶ່ງຊິ່ງມີສອງເມຍ. ເມຍໂຕທີໜຶ່ງຢູ່ບະຄອງນຳປີ ແລະ ເມຍໂຕທີສອງຢູ່ບະຄອງ ນາລາ. ມັນເອງຢູ່ສະຖານທີບ່ອຍແທ່ງທີ່ງລະຫວ່າງນຳປີ ແລະ ນາລາ. ບາງເທື່ອມັນກໍໄປຫາເມຍຢູ່ນຳປີ ແລະ ບາງເທື່ອກໍໄປຫາເມຍຢູ່ນາລາ.

ຄັ້ງໜຶ່ງກົບນ້ອຍໂຕໜຶ່ງໄດ້ມາຫາມັນ ແລະ ກໍເວົ້າວ່າ, "ຂໍເຊີນທ່ານເມືອນຳປີ! ເມຍຜູ້ທີໜຶ່ງຂອງທ່ານເຮັດເຂົ້າໜົມພຸດດິງສຳລັບທ່ານ."

ກົບໂຕນັ້ນດີໃຈຫລາຍ, ເພາະວ່າມັນມັກເຂົ້າໜົມພຸດດິງແທ້ໆ, ມັນກຽມພ້ອມທີຈະໄປໃນຂະນະກົບນ້ອຍໂຕໜຶ່ງອີກມາຫາມັນ ແລະ ກໍເວົ້າວ່າ, "ຂໍເຊີນທ່ານເມືອນາລາ! ເມຍຜູ້ທີສອງຂອງທ່ານເຮັດເຂົ້າໜົມພຸດດິງສຳລັບທ່ານ. ເຊີນເມືອໂລດໃນຂະນະທີ່ເຂົ້າໜົມພຸດດິງ ພວມຮ້ອນຢູ່ນີ້."

ກົບໂຕນັ້ນບໍ່ງລົງ ແລະ ເລີ່ມຄິດ, "ຖ້າວ່າຂ້າພະເຈົ້າໄປຫາເມຍຜູ້ທີ່ໜຶ່ງເພື່ອເຂົ້າໜົມພຸດດິງນັ້ນ, ເມຍຜູ້ທີສອງຂອງຂ້າພະເຈົ້າຈະເສຍໃຈ ແລະ ຄຽດໄຫ້. ຖ້າວ່າຂ້າພະເຈົ້າໄປຫາເມຍຜູ້ທີສອງເພື່ອເຂົ້າໜົມພຸດດິ້ງເມຍຜູ້ທີ່ໜຶ່ງຂອງຂ້າພະເຈົ້າຈະເສຍໃຈ ແລະ ຄຽດຄືກັນ. ຂ້າພະເຈົ້າຈະໄປໃສເດີ່-ໄປນຳປີຫລີໄປນາລາທວະ?

ມັນບໍ່ງ ແລະ ຄິດຄິນເຕີບ. ມັນພັກຢູ່ເຮືອນ ແລະ ກໍເລີ່ມຮ້ອງໄຫ້ຂຶ້ນ, "ໂອ! ຂ້າພະເຈົ້າຈະໄປໃສເດີ່, ຂ້າພະເຈົ້າຈະໄປໃສເດີ່?".

Shapes and Sounds

จีบเถิงปะจุบัน, เมื່อท่านได้ยินกับร้อງ, "ອິບ! ອິບ! ອິບ!" ท่านจะเຂົ້າใจได้อ่ามันหมายเถิງ: "ข้าพะเจ้าจะ ไปใสเดบ๊? ไปบ่? ไปบ่? ไปบ่?."
เป็บทาบบ่ดิแท้ๆมั ที่มีสอງเมยซึ່ງເຮັດເຂົ້າໜົມພຸດ ດຶງໃນເວລາດຽວກັນ!"

Once there lived a frog who had two wives. His first wife lived in Nambi and the second wife live in Nala. He himself lived in a little place between Nambi and Nala. Sometimes he went to Nambi and sometimes to Nala to see his wives.

Once a little frog came to him and said, "Come to Nambi, please! Your first wife has made pudding for you. Come at once while the pudding is hot!"

The frog was very happy because he liked pudding very much. He was ready to go when another little frog came up to him and said, "Please come to Nala! Your second wife has made pudding for you. Come at once while the pudding is hot!"

The frog sat down and began to think, "If I go to my first wife for the pudding, my second wife will be sorry and angry. If I go to my second wife for the pudding, my first wife will be sorry and angry, too. Where shall I go—to Nambi or Nala?"

He sat and thought for a long time. He stayed at home and began to cry, "Oh! Where shall I go? Where shall I go?"

Now, when you hear a frog's "Awp! Awp! Awp!" you will understand that it means: "Where shall I go? Shall I go? Shall I go? Shall I go?"

How bad it is to have two wives who make pudding at the same time!

T 87 How the Dog and the Chicken Became Domestic Animals

หมาและไก่ได้กายเป็บสัดบ้าบได้แบวใด

มีถั่ງໜຶ່ງ ໃນເມື່ອນີກຈຳພວກໜຶ່ງ ແລະ ສັດ ຈຳພວກໜຶ່ງອາໄສຢູ່ເທິງທ້ອງຟ້າ. ສ່ວນໝາ ແລະ ໄກ່ກຳລາ ໄສຢູ່ທີ່ມັນຄືກັນ.

Shapes and Sounds

ມື້ໜຶ່ງຢູ່ເທິງທ້ອງຟ້າອາກາດໜາວ ແລະ ຝົນຕົກ. ນົກ ທັງຫຼາຍໄດ້ຮ້ອງຂໍໃຫ້ໝາໂຕໜຶ່ງລົງໄປໂລກມະນຸດເພື່ອ ເອົາໄຟມາໃຫ້ທ້ອງຟ້າອົບອຸ່ນ.

ໝາໂຕນັ້ນກໍລົງໄປແລ້ວກໍມາເຖິງເຮືອນຂອງຊາຍ ຄົນໜຶ່ງ. ໝາຫຼາຍເຫັນກອງກະດູກຢູ່ໃກ້ກັບເຮືອນຫຼັງ ນັ້ນ. ມັນກໍເລີຍກິນກະດູກແລ້ວກໍລືມນົກແລະໄຟເສຍເລີຍ.

ນົກທັງຫຼາຍລໍຖ້າໝາໂຕນັ້ນ, ແຕ່ມັນກໍບໍ່ກັບມາເລີຍ. ມັນຕັດສິນໃຈຢູ່ກັບຊາຍຄົນນັ້ນ.

ໃນຂະນະນັ້ນອາກາດກໍຍັງໜາວຢູ່,ນົກທັງຫຼາຍ ກໍສົ່ງໄກ່ໂຕໜຶ່ງລົງໄປເອົາໄຟມາ. ໄກ່ໂຕນັ້ນກໍໄປເຖິງ ເຮືອນຂອງຊາຍຄົນໜຶ່ງ ແລະກໍຫຼຽວເຫັນເມັດເຂົ້າ ຢູ່ໃກ້ກັບເຮືອນຫຼັງນັ້ນ. ມັນມັກເມັດເຂົ້າຫຼາຍທີ່ສຸດ. ໄກ່ໂຕນັ້ນບໍ່ໄດ້ຄິດເຖິງໄຟເລີຍ, ມີແຕ່ກິນເມັດເຂົ້າເທົ່ານັ້ນ. ແລ້ວມັນກໍຕັດສິນໃຈຢູ່ກັບຊາຍຄົນນັ້ນເໝືອນກັນ.

ດ້ວຍເຫດນັ້ນນົກ ແລະ ສັດທັງຫຼາຍຈຶ່ງບໍ່ມັກໝາ ແລະ ໄກ່: ພວກມັນຈາກໝູ່ເພື່ອນຂອງຕົນທີ່ຢູ່ໃນຄວາມ ໜາວໄປ ເພື່ອເຫັນແກ່ອາຫານດີໆເທົ່ານັ້ນ. ຈົນເຖິງປັດຈຸ ບັນນີ້ພວກທ່ານຈຶ່ງຮູ້ໄດ້ວ່າໝາ ແລະ ໄກ່ໄດ້ກາຍມາ ເປັນສັດບ້ານແລ້ວ.

There was a time when some birds and some animals lived in the sky. The dog and the hen lived there, too. One day it was very cold and rainy in the sky. The birds asked the dog to go down to the earth and bring some fire to make the sky warm.

The dog went down and came to a man's house. He saw many bones near the house. He began to eat the bones and forgot about the birds and the fire.

The birds waited and waited for the dog, but he did not come back. He decided to live with the man.

Shapes and Sounds

As it was still cold, the birds sent the hen down to bring some fire. The hen went to the man's house and saw some seeds near the house. She liked the seeds very much. The hen did not think about the fire, but ate up the seeds. She decided to live with the man, too.

That is why the birds and the animals do not like the dog and the hen. They left their friends in the cold for the sake of good food. Now you know how the dog and the hen became domestic animals.

T 88 The Cat and her Strong Friends

ແມວ ແລະ ເພື່ອນທີ່ແຂງແຮງຂອງມັນ

ດັ່ງທີ່ງມີແມວໂຕໜຶ່ງອາໄສຢູ່ແຖ່ງໜຶ່ງ, ມັນຄິດວ່າ, "ສິງເປັນສັດທີ່ແຂງແຮງກວ່າໝູ່ໝົດ. ເປັນການດີແລ້ວທີ່ມີເພື່ອນທີ່ແຂງແຮງເຊັ່ນນີ້. ກູຈະໄປຫາສິງແລ້ວເປັນເພື່ອນກັບມັນ." ແມວກໍເຣັດດັ່ງທີ່ຄິດໄວ້, ສິງ ແລະ ແມວກໍເປັນເພື່ອນກັນມາຕັ້ງຫລາຍໆວັນ.

ດັ່ງທີ່ງພວກມັນພາກັນໄປຢ່າງທລົ້ນ ແລະ ໄດ້ພົບກັບຊ້າງໂຕໜຶ່ງ. ສິງກໍເລີ້ມຕີກັນກັບຊ້າງ, ແລ້ວຊ້າງກໍຂ້າສິງຕາຍ. ອ້າຍແມວກໍເສຍໃຈຫລາຍພ້ອມທັງຄິດວ່າ: "ກູຈະເຣັດແນວໃດບາດນີ້, ຊ້າງແຮງກວ່າສິງ. ກູຈະໄປຫາຊ້າງເພື່ອເປັນເພື່ອນກັບມັນ". ແມວກໍເຣັດດັ່ງທີ່ຄິດໄວ້, ພວກມັນກໍເປັນເພື່ອນກັນມາຕັ້ງຫລາຍໆ ວັນ.

ດັ່ງທີ່ງພວກມັນພາກັນໄປຢ່າງທລົ້ນ ແລະກໍພົບກັບນາຍພານຄົນໜຶ່ງ. ນາຍພານຄົນນັ້ນກໍເລີຍຍິງຊ້າງຕາຍ. ອ້າຍແມວກໍຍິ່ງເສຍໃຈພ້ອມທັງຄິດວ່າ, "ຊາຍຄົນນັ້ນແຮງກວ່າຊ້າງກູເທີນແລ້ວ". ດັ່ງນັ້ນແມວຈຶ່ງຢ່າງໄປຫານາຍພານ ແລະ ຮ້ອງຂຶ້ນວ່າ, "ຂ້ອຍຂໍໄປນຳແມ່ໄດ້ບໍ?"

ນາຍພານເລີຍເວົ້າວ່າ, "ກໍແລ້ວພວກເຮົາເມືອເຮືອນເທາະ."

Shapes and Sounds

ພວກເຂົາມາຮອດເຮືອນຂາຍຕິນບັ້ນ. ເມຍຂອງລາວ
ເຫັນ ແລະ ກຳເອົາປືນບຳລາວ. ອ້າຍແມວທລຽວເຫັນກຳຄິດ
ວ່າ, "ໂອ, ຜູ້ຍິງແຂງແຮງກວ່າທຸກສິ່ງນໍ! ລາວຈິ່ງສາມາດ
ເອົາປືນອອກຈາກນາຍພານໄດ້, ແລ້ວນາຍພານກໍບໍ່ຕິເມຍ
ເລີຍ, ແມ່ນແຕ່ຄຳໜຶ່ງລາວກໍບໍ່ເວົ້າໃຫ້ເລີຍ!"
ຂາຍຕິນບັ້ນນັ່ງອົງໂຕະ, ແລະ ຍິງຕິນບັ້ນກຳໄປ
ເຮືອນຄົວ ແມວກຳໄປເຮືອນຄົວຄືກັນມັນຕັດສິນໃຈຢູ່ກັບ
ຜູ້ຍິງຕະຫລອດໄປ. ດ້ວຍເຫດນັ້ນພວກທ່ານຈິ່ງເຫັນແມວ
ຢູ່ໃກ້ ຊິດຕິດຕີນຂອງຜູ້ຍິງຢູ່ເຮືອນຄົວສະເໝີໄປ.

Once there lived a cat. She thought, "The lion is the strongest of all the animals. It is good to have strong friends. I shall go to the lion and make friends with him." She did so, and the lion and the cat were friends for many, many days.

Once they went for a walk together and met an elephant. The lion began to fight with the elephant and the elephant killed him. The cat felt very bad. She thought to herself, "What shall I do? The elephant was stronger than the lion. I shall go to the elephant and make friends with him." She did so and they were friends for many, many days.

Once they went for a walk and met a hunter. The hunter shot the elephant and killed him. The cat felt very bad, but she thought, "The man is stronger than the elephant, I see." So she went up to the hunter and asked, "May I go with you?"

He said, "All right, let us go home together."

They came to the man's house. His wife met him and took his gun from him. The cat saw that and thought, "Oh, the woman is the strongest of all! She can take the hunter's gun from him and he does not fight with her. He does not even say a word!"

The man sat down at the table and the woman went to the kitchen. The cat went to the kitchen, too. She decided to stay with the woman forever. That is why you always see a cat in the kitchen at a woman's feet.

T 89 Why the Crocodile Does Not Eat Hens

ເປັນຫຍັງແຂ້ຈິ່ງບໍ່ກິນໄກ່ແມ່

ມີໄກ່ແມ່ໂຕນຶ່ງໄດ້ມາເຖິງແມ່ນ້ຳທຸກໆມື້. ມັນດື່ມນ້ຳ
ຢູ່ທັ້ນ, ມື້ນຶ່ງແຂ້ໂຕນຶ່ງຫລຽວເຫັນແລ້ວກໍມາຫາມັນ.
ແຂ້ຢາກກິນໄກ່ໂຕນັ້ນ. ໄກ່ເລີຍຮ້ອງໄຫ້ຂຶ້ນວ່າ, "ໂອຍ, ຢ່າ
ຊິກິນຂ້ານ້ອຍທ້ອນອ້າຍທີ່ຮັກເອີຍ!" ແຂ້ກໍປ່ອຍໃຫ້ມັນໄປ,
ແຂ້ບໍ່ກິນນ້ອງສາວຂອງຕົນ!

ມື້ຕໍ່ມາເມື່ອໄກ່ມາເຖິງແມ່ນ້ຳອີກ, ແຂ້ກໍຕັດສິນໃຈວ່າ
ຊິກິນມັນແທ້ໆ. ແຕ່ວ່າໄກ່ກໍຮ້ອງໄຫ້ຂຶ້ນຄືເກົ່າ, "ໂອຍ, ຢ່າ
ຊິກິນຂ້ານ້ອຍທ້ອນອ້າຍທີ່ຮັກເອີຍ!" ແຂ້ກໍບໍ່ກິນມັນອີກ.

ແຕ່ມັນກໍຄິດວ່າ, "ກູເປັນອ້າຍຂອງມັນໄດ້ຢ່າງໃດ? ກູຢູ່
ນ້ຳ ແລະ ມັນຢູ່ບົກ". ຫລັງຈາກນັ້ນແຂ້ກໍໄປຫາເພື່ອນຂອງ
ມັນຄືຈໍໂພະ.

"ໂອ, ສະຫາຍເອີຍ! ໄກ່ແມ່ບັກໃຫຍ່ມາເຖິງແມ່ນ້ຳ
ທຸກໆມື້ແລ້ວເຮົາຢາກກິນມັນ, ມັນເລີຍເວົ້າວ່າເຮົາ
ເປັນອ້າຍຂອງມັນ. ເປັນໄດ້ຢ່າງໃດບໍ?"

ຈໍໂພະຕອບວ່າ: "ໂອ, ບັກຈ້າເອີຍ. ໂຕຮູ້ບໍ່ວ່າໄກ່,
ເຕົ່າ, ຈໍໂພະອອກໄຂ່ຄືກັບແຂ້ນັ້ນແລ້ວເພື່ອນຮັກເອີຍ?
ດັ່ງນັ້ນພວກເຮົາທັງໝົດຈິ່ງເປັນອ້າຍເອື້ອຍນ້ອງກັນ. ໂຕ
ເຂົ້າໃຈແລ້ວບໍ?"

ແຂ້ເວົ້າວ່າ: "ໂອ, ຂອບໃຈຫລາຍໆເດີ".
ຈົນເຖິງປັດຈຸບັນນີ້ພວກທ່ານຈິ່ງໄດ້ຮູ້ສາຍເຫດທີ່ແຂ້
ບໍ່ເຄີຍກິນໄກ່ຈັກເທື່ອເລີຍ!

A hen came to the river every day. She drank water there. One day the crocodile saw her and came up to her. He wanted to eat her up. But she cried, "Don't eat me, my dear brother!" The crocodile let her go. He could not eat his sister.

Shapes and Sounds

The next day, when the hen came to the river again, the crocodile decided to eat her up. But again the hen cried, "Oh, don't eat me, my dear brother!" And again the crocodile didn't eat her.

But he thought to himself, "How can I be her brother? I live in the water and she doesn't." Then the crocodile went to his friend, a lizard.

"Oh, my friend! A big hen comes to the river every day and when I want to catch her, she says that I am her brother. How can that be?"

The lizard answered, "Oh my silly friend! Don't you know that the hen, the turtle and the lizard lay eggs as crocodiles do? So we all are brothers and sisters. Do you understand?"

The crocodile said, "Oh, thank you very much."

Now you know why crocodiles never eat hens.

T 90 Why the Hawk Eats Chicks

ເປັນຫຍັງແຫລວຈິ່ງກິນໄກ່ນ້ອຍ

ຄັ້ງໜຶ່ງລູກແຫລວໂຕໜຶ່ງໄຂ້ແຮງ. ນ້ອງສາວຂອງແຫລວຈິ່ງໄດ້ມາທາງແຫລວ ແລະ ເວົ້າວ່າ, "ຂ້ອຍຮູ້ທ່ານໜໍ ທີ່ດີສຳລັບລູກເຈົ້າ. ແມງມູມເປັນທ່ານໜໍທີ່ດີທີ່ສຸດຢູ່ທີ່ນີ້. ຂ້ອຍຈະໄປອ້ອນວອນເພິ່ນມາຫາເຈົ້າເດີ".

ແມ່ແຫລວໄດ້ໃຫ້ນ້ອງສາວຂອງຕົນໄປຫາທ່ານໜໍ ຜູ້ນັ້ນ. ນ້ອງສາວຂອງລາວກໍໄປຫາແມງມູມແລະເວົ້າວ່າ, "ແຫລວມີລູກໂຕໜຶ່ງ ແລະ ມັນເປັນໄຂ້ແຮງ. ທ່ານໜໍຈະໄປຫາແຫລວ ແລະ ເບິ່ງລູກຂອງລາວແມ່ໄດ້ບໍ?"

ແມງມູມເວົ້າວ່າ, "ດີແລ້ວ, ແຕ່ວ່າຂ້ອຍຢ້ານ. ທີ່ນັ້ນມີໄກ່ແມ່ໂຕໜຶ່ງຢູ່ໃຫ້ກັບເຮືອນຂອງແຫລວ ແລະ ມັນຊິກິນຂ້ອຍ."

ນ້ອງສາວຂອງແຫລວເວົ້າວ່າ, "ໂອ, ບໍ່, ຂ້ອຍເຊື່ອວ່າມັນບໍ່ກິນເຈົ້າດອກ."

ດັ່ງນັ້ນ ແມງມູມຈິ່ງເອົາແກ້ວຢາຂອງລາວໃສ່ໃນຖົງ

Shapes and Sounds

ພາຍແລ້ວກໍໄປຫາແຫລວ,
ແຕ່ລາວກໍຍັງຢ້ານໄກ່ແມ່ໂຕນັ້ນຢູ່, ດັ່ງນັ້ນລາວ
ຈິ່ງຂໍຮັບສິໃສ່ຕີງພາຍພ້ອມກັບ ແກ້ວຢາ.
ທັນໃດນັ້ນລາວຫລວງເຫັນໄກ່ແມ່ໂຕນັ້ນ!
ລາວຈິ່ງລີ້ຢູ່ຂ້າງຕົ້ນໄມ້, ແຕ່ວ່າ ໄກ່ແມ່ພັດຫລວງເຫັນ
ແມງມູມແລ້ວເອົາມັນໄປໃຫ້ລູກກິນ.

ແຫລວຕອດໂຕນັ້ນກໍຖ້າແລ້ວຖ້າຢູ່. ບາດແລ້ວລາວ
ກໍຍ່າງອອກໄປຫາແມງມູມ ແລະກໍເຫັນແຕ່ຕີງພາຍທັງ
ແກ້ວຢາ ແລະຫັງສິຢູ່ທັນ. ລາວເລີຍອ່ານ, "ເຖິງແຫລວ ຜູ້
ຂ້າໄດ້ເດີນທາງເພື່ອໄປເຮືອນຂອງທ່ານ, ເມື່ອຜູ້ຂ້າໄດ້ເຫັນ
ໄກ່ແມ່ໂຕນັ້ນມັນກໍເລີຍກິນຜູ້ຂ້າຊຳ້."

ແຫລວໂຕນັ້ນກໍບິນກັບໄປຫາລູກຊາຍຂອງຕົນ,
ທັນໃດນັ້ນລູກຊາຍກໍເລີຍຕາຍຢ່າງໜ້າສັງເວດແຫລວ ກໍຕົກ
ລົງໃຈໄປແກ້ແຄ້ນແລ້ວກໍກິນລູກໄກ່ໝົດທຸກໂຕເລີຍ.

ຈົນເຖິງປັດຈຸບັນນີ້ ແຫລວຈິ່ງຫຍູມເອົາລູກ
ໄກ່ໄປກິນຢູ່ສະເໝີ, ເມື່ອພວກທ່ານຈັບ ໄກ່ແມ່,
ມັນຈິ່ງຮ້ອງອອກມາວ່າ, "ບໍ່ແມ່ນຂ້ອຍ! ບໍ່ແມ່ນຂ້ອຍ!"
ມັນຢາກເວົ້າວ່າ, "ຂ້ອຍບໍ່ໄດ້ກິນແມງມູມ! ບໍ່ແມ່ນຂ້ອຍ!
ບໍ່ແມ່ນຂ້ອຍ!"

Once the Hawk's child was very ill. The Hawk's sister came to Mother Hawk and said, "I know a good doctor for your child. The Spider is the best doctor here. I shall ask him to come to you."

Mother Hawk asked her sister to go for the doctor. Her sister went to the Spider and said, "The Hawk has a child who is very ill. Will you go to the Hawk and see her child?"

The Spider said, "All right, but I am afraid to go. There lives a Hen near the Hawk's house and she will eat me up."

The Hawk's sister said, "Oh, no, I am sure she won't eat you up."

So the Spider took his medicine bottles, put them in a bag and went to the Hawk. But he was afraid of the Hen. So he wrote a letter and put it into the bag with the medicine bottles. Very soon he saw the Hen! He hid himself behind a tree. But the Hen saw the Spider, picked him up and gave him to her chicks to eat.

Now the Hawk waited and waited for the Spider. Then she went out to meet him and saw a bag with medicine bottles and a letter there. She read, "To the Hawk: I was on my way to your house when I met the Hen who ate me up."

The Hawk flew back to her little son. The poor child soon died. The Hawk decided to take revenge and began to eat chicks. Now the Hawk always catches chicks and eats them.

When you catch a hen it cries out, "It was not I! It was not I!" She wants to say, "I did not eat the Spider! It was not I! It was not I!"

T 91 Why the Lizard Shakes His Head

ດ້ວຍເຫດໃດກະປອມຈຶ່ງງຶກຫົວຂອງມັນ

ດົນນານຜ່ານມາແລ້ວກະປອມແລະໝາໄດ້ເປັນໝູ່ເພື່ອນກັນ. ແຕ່ບາງເທື່ອ ໝາກໍໄປຢ່າງຫລົ້ນກັບຜູ້ຂາຍຕົ້ມນັນ. ມີຫນຶ່ງກະປອມໄດ້ຖາມໝາວ່າ, "ເປັນຫຍັງບາງເທື່ອເຈົ້າກໍໄປກັບຂາຍຕົ້ມນັນ?"

ໝາຕອບວ່າ, "ຂາຍຕົ້ມນັນ ແລະຂ້ອຍເປັນເພື່ອນກັນ, ຂາຍຕົ້ມນັນເປັນນາຍພານແລະພວກຂ້ອຍໄປປ່າເນືອງກັນ. ຂ້ອຍລ່າເນື້ອຊ່ວຍລາວ, ເມື່ອພວກຂ້ອຍກັບມາພວກຂ້ອຍໄດ້ຊີ້ນມານຳແລ້ວພວກຂ້ອຍກໍກິນຊິ້ນນັນ."

ຄັ້ງຫນຶ່ງຂາຍຕົ້ມນັນ ແລະ ໝາໄດ້ໄປປ່າລ່າເນື້ອ. ພວກເຂົາຊ້າເຢັນໄດ້ໂຕຫນຶ່ງແລ້ວກໍຫາມມາເຮືອນຂອງນາຍພານນັ້ນ. ກະປອມຫລຽວເຫັນພວກເຂົາແລ້ວກໍຕິດຕາມພວກເຂົາໄປ. ນາຍພານໄດ້ເອົາຊິ້ນນັ້ນມາແຕ່ງກິນເປັນອາຫານຄຳ. ໝາໂຕນັ້ນກໍມາຫາຂາຍຕົ້ມນັນ ແລະ ກໍຢາກໄດ້ຊິ້ນຈຳນວນຫນຶ່ງຕິກັນ. ບາດແລ້ວນາຍພານ

Shapes and Sounds

ຈຶ່ງລາກເອົາໄມ້ຄ້ອນບັກໃຫຍ່ມາຕີທິວໝາໂຕນັ້ນ!
ໝາກໍເລັຽຮ້ອງໄຫ້ຢ່າງໜ້າສັງເວດ ແລ້ວກໍແລ່ນໜີໄປ.
ກະປອມທລວງເຫັນທຸກຢ່າງແລ້ວມັນກໍ
ແລ່ນໜີໄປເໝືອນກັນ, ມັນແລ່ນເຂົ້າໄປໃນປ່າ
ຢຸດຢູ່ທີ່ນັ້ນແລ້ວງຶກທິວຂອງມັນ. ມັນຮ້ອງຂຶ້ນວ່າ, "ແຈງກູ!
ແຈງກູ! ແຈງກູ! ຂໍ້ພິລິກ ແທ້ນໍ! ເປັນຫຍັງໝາຈຶ່ງເວົ້າໄດ້
ວ່າມັນເປັນເພື່ອນຂອງນາຍພານ, ມັນລ່າເບື້ອຊ່ວຍລາວ
ແລະເອົາຂຶ້ນ ມາບັກທລາຍໆ ແລ້ວນາຍພານຜູ້ນັ້ນຈຶ່ງ
ເອົາໄມ້ຄ້ອນຕີທິວໝາຢ່າງໜ້າສັງເວດ! ຂາຍຄົນນັ້ນບໍ່ດີ,
ກູຈະບໍ່ຢູ່ໃກ້ມັນ. ກູຈະໄປຢູ່ໃນປ່າພຸ້ນ!"
ອັນນັ້ນເປັນສາຍເຫດເຮັດໃຫ້ກະປອມອາໄສຢູ່ໃນ
ປ່າ ຂຶ້ງຫ່າງຈາກເຮືອນຄົນ. ເມື່ອມັນຄິດເຫັນຂາຍຄົນນັ້ນ
ແລະ ໄມ້ຄ້ອນໃຫຍ່ຂອງລາວມັນຈຶ່ງງຶກທິວ ແລະ ເວົ້າວ່າ,
"ແຈງກູ! ແຈງກູ! ແຈງກູ! ຂໍ້ພິລິກແທ້ນໍ! ຂໍ້ພິລິກແທ້ນໍ!
ຂໍ້ພິລິກແທ້ນໍ!"

Long, long ago the Chameleon and the Dog were friends. But sometimes the Dog walked with the man. One day the Chameleon asked the Dog, "Why do you sometimes go with the man?"

The Dog answered, "The man and I are friends. The man is a hunter, and we go hunting together. I help him to hunt. We have meat when we come back. Then we eat it."

Once the man and the Dog went hunting. They killed an antelope and carried it to the hunter's house. The Chameleon saw them and followed them. The hunter made dinner from the meat and began to eat it. The Dog came up to the man and wanted to have some meat, too. The hunter took a big stick and hit the Dog on the head! The poor Dog cried and ran away.

The Chameleon saw everything and he ran away, too. He ran into the forest, stopped there and began to shake his head. He cried, "Chengu! Chengu! Chengu! That's too bad! Why, the Dog says he is the hunter's friend. He helps him to hunt and brings him meat. And the hunter hits the poor Dog on the head with a stick! The man is not good. I will not live near the man. I will live in the forest!"

That is why the Chameleon lives in the forest far from the home of the man. When he thinks of the man and his big stick he shakes his head and says, "Chengu! Chengu! Chengu! Too bad! Too bad! Too bad!"

T 92 The Lost Son ລູກຊາຍທີ່ເສຍ

ຄັ້ງນຶ່ງມີຊາຍຄົນນຶ່ງທີ່ມີລູກຊາຍຢູ່ສອງຄົນ. ຜູ້ນ້ອງເວົ້າກັບພໍ່ວ່າ, "ພໍ່ເອີຍ, ຈົ່ງເອົາຊັບສົມບັດທີ່ຈະ ຕົກເປັນຂອງລູກນັ້ນ ໃຫ້ລູກດຽວນີ້ສາ." ດັ່ງນັ້ນ ພໍ່ຈຶ່ງໄດ້ ແບ່ງຊັບສົມໃຫ້ລູກຊາຍທັງສອງຂອງຕົນ. ຕໍ່ມາບໍ່ພໍເທົ່າໃດ ມີຜູ້ເປັນນ້ອງກໍ່ໄດ້ຂາຍຊັບສົມທີ່ຕົກເປັນ ສ່ວນຂອງຕົນນັ້ນ ແລະ ຈາກບ້ານໄປພ້ອມດ້ວຍເງິນ. ລາວໜີໄປຍັງແດນໄກ ແລະ ຜານຊັບຂອງຕົນຢູ່ທີ່ນັ້ນໃນທາງຢູ່ກິນຍ່າງໆ ຂາດລະບຽບ. ລາວໄດ້ຈັບຈ່າຍຊັບຈົນໝົດກ້ຽງ. ຕໍ່ ມາກໍເກີດການອົດຢາກອັນຮ້າຍແຮງທົ່ວ ປະເທດ ແລະ ລາວບໍ່ມີຫຍັງເຫຼືອຢູ່ເລີຍ. ດັ່ງນັ້ນລາວ ຈຶ່ງໄປຂໍຮັບຈ້າງນຳຄົນນຶ່ງໃນ ເມືອງນັ້ນ ແລະ ຄົນນີ້ກໍ ໃຊ້ລາວອອກໄປລ້ຽງໝູທີ່ທົ່ງນາ. ລາວຄິດຢາກ ກິນຝັກຖົ່ວທີ່ໝູກິນ ໃຫ້ອີ່ມທ້ອງແຕ່ບໍ່ມີໃຜເອົາ ໃຫ້ລາວກິນ. ໃນທີ່ສຸດລາວກໍສຳນຶກຕົວໄດ້ ແລະເວົ້າກັບ ຕົນເອງວ່າ, "ລູກຈ້າງທຸກຄົນຂອງ ພໍ່ຂ້ອຍກໍຍັງມີອາຫານ ກິນຈົນເຫຼືອເຝືອ ສ່ວນຂ້ອຍພວມຕາຍຫິວຢູ່ທີ່ນີ້! ຂ້ອຍຈະລຸກຂຶ້ນເມືອຫາພໍ່ຂອງຂ້ອຍ ແລະເວົ້າວ່າ, "ພໍ່ເອີຍ, ລູກໄດ້ເຮັດບາບຕໍ່ພະເຈົ້າແລະຕໍ່ພໍ່ແລ້ວ, ລູກບໍ່ສົມຄວນທີ່ ຂ້ອ່າເປັນລູກຂອງພໍ່ອີກຕໍ່ໄປ; ຈົ່ງເຮັດກັບລູກຄືລູກຈ້າງຄົນ

ทั่งของพํ่." ดั่งนั้น ลาวจิ่งลุกขึ้นຄືนเมือทาพํ่ของตืน.

ຂະນະทີ่ยัງอยู่ท่างไກจากบ้านพํ่สົມຄວນ พํ่ກຳແນມ
เຫັນลาว ແລະสิ่งสานจิ่งแล่นออกไปกอดลูกไว้ด้วย
ความรักแพງ, ผู้เป็นลูกจิ่งเว้าว่า, "พํ่เฮີย, ลูกได้
เຮັดบาบต่อพະเจ้า ແລະต่อพํ่แล้ว, ลูกบํ่สົມควນที่ຊິ່ว่า
เป็นลูกของพํ่อີກต่อไป." แต่ผู้เป็นพํ່เอິ้นบັນดาคົນใຊ้
ของตนมา, เพິ່นเว้าว่า, "ไวๆ รับเอົາเคื่อງย่าງดีที่สุด
มาใຫ້ลูกของเฮົາนຸ່ງ. จิ່ງเอົາแทอบมาสวມใส่นิ້วมື
ແລະสุບເກີບใส่ตืນใຫ້ลูกของเฮົາ. ແລ້ວจิ່ງไปเอົາງົວ
ຫນຸ່ມໂຕຕຸ້ຍພີ່ດີງາມມາຂ້າ ແລະจัดງານກິນລ້ຽງຂຶ້ນຮ່ວມ
ກັບສະຫລອງ! ด้วยว่าลูกเฮົາຄືນมีตายแล້ว แต่บัດ
นี้ลาวมีຊີວິດอยู่; ลาวเสยไปแล้ว แต่บัດนี้เຮົາได้ພົບ
ลาวอีก." สะบับแทละງານກິນລ້ຽງ จิ່ງเลີ່มขึ້น.

ใນละຫວ່າງนั้นลูกຊາຍผู้พิ่ກຳอยู่ที่ທີ່ງມາ. ตอนกັບ
มาเมื่อใຫ້จะรอดเຮືອนลาวได้ຍືนສຽງເພງ ແລະສຽງ
คืนพ້ອມຟ້ອນລຳ. ดั่งนั้น ลาวจิ่งເອີ້นคืนใຊ้ผู้หนึ่ງ มา
ແລະຖາມว่า, "มีຫຍັງເກີດขึ้น?" คืนใຊ້ผู้นັ້นตอบว่า:
"น້ອງຊາຍของท่านกັບมาแล้ว ແລະพํ่ของท່ານได้
ຂ້າງົວຫນຸ່ມໂຕຕຸ້ຍພີ່ດີງາມ เพາະเพิ່นได้ลาวຄືນมาย่าງ
สะຫວັດດິພາບ."

ฝ่ายอ້າຍກໍໂກດຮ້າຍໃຫຍ່. ຈຶ່ງບໍ່ຍອມເຂົ້າມາ
ໃນເຮືອນ; ดั่งนั้นผู້ເປັນພໍ່ຈຶ່ງອອກໄປວິງວອນໃຫ້ເຂົ້າມາ.
แต่ลาวเว้าคืนใຫ້พํ່ว่า, "เບິ່ງແມ! ลูกได้เຮັດວຽກใຫ້
พํ່ດั່ງທາດຕະຫລອດມາຫລາຍປີ ແລະลูกบํ່เคีຍฝ่าຜືນຄຳ
สั່ງของพํ່จักเທື່ອ, พํ่ได้ใຫ້ຫຍັງລูກແດ່? บํ่ใຫ້ຫຍັງເລີຍ
ແມ່ນແຕ່ລູກແບ້ໂຕດຽວກໍບໍ່ໃຫ້ເພື່ອจัดງານສັງສັນກັບໝູ່

ເພື່ອນ! ແຕ່ເມື່ອລູກຊາຍຂອງພໍ່ຄົນນີ້ ຜູ້ທີ່ໄດ້ຜານຊັບ
ສິນທັງໝົດຂອງພໍ່ດ້ວຍການຄົບຫາກັບພວກໂສເພນີຄືນມາ
ເຮືອນແລ້ວ ພໍ່ຂາໍພັດຂ້າງົວເຖິກໂຕທີ່ດີສຸດລ້ຽງລາວ!"
ຜູ້ເປັນພໍ່ຕອບວ່າ, "ລູກເອີຍ, ເຈົ້າຢູ່ກັບພໍ່ທີ່ນີ້ສະເໝີ
ແລະທຸກໆ ສິ່ງທີ່ພໍ່ມີກໍເປັນຂອງລູກ. ແຕ່ພວກເຮົາຈຳ
ເປັນຕ້ອງຮ່ວມສະຫລອງ ແລະດີໃຈນຳກັນ ເພາະນ້ອງຂອງ
ເຈົ້າຕາຍແລ້ວ ແຕ່ບັດນີ້ມີຊີວິດຢູ່; ລາວເສຍໄປແລ້ວ ແຕ່
ບັດນີ້ເຮົາໄດ້ພົບລາວອີກ."

Once there was a man who had two sons. The younger son said to his father, "Father, give me my inheritance—the part that will fall to your son—give it to your son now." Therefore, the father divided the inheritance and gave it to his two sons. Some time later the younger son sold the inheritance that fell to him and left home with the money. He went to a faraway land and wasted his inheritance there in a lawless manner. He spent all that he had. Then there was a severe famine over the whole country and he had nothing left. Therefore, he went to work for one man in that city and this man sent him out to his fields to raise pigs. He thought about how he wanted to eat the bean pods that the pigs were filling their stomachs with, but no one gave them to him to eat. Finally, he came to his senses and said to himself, "All of my father's hired men have food to eat and more, and here I am dying of thirst. I will get up and return to my father and say, 'Dear father, I have sinned against God and against you. I should not be called your son anymore. Make me like one of your hired men.'" Therefore he got up and returned to his father.

But when he was still pretty far from his house his father saw him and pitied him, so he ran out and hugged his son tightly with love. The son said, "Dear father, I have sinned against God and against you. I should not be called your son anymore." But the father called all his servants to him. He said, "Quickly! Bring the nicest clothes here and give them to my son to wear. Bring a ring and put it on his finger and put shoes on the feet of my son. Then, go get the young, fat, nice-looking calf, kill it and prepare a feast for us to celebrate! Because this son of mine died already, but now he is living; he was lost but now I have found him again!" Therefore the feast began.

Meanwhile, the oldest son was in the fields. When he returned close to home he heard the sound of music and people dancing. Therefore, he called one of the servants and asked him, "What has happened?" The servant answered, "Your younger brother has returned and your father has killed the young, fat, nice-looking calf because he has gotten him back safe and sound."

The older brother became very angry and refused to enter the house. Therefore, the father had to come out and plead with him to enter. But he talked back to his father, "Look here! I have worked for you like a slave throughout many years and I have never disobeyed your orders. And what have you given to me? You haven't given me anything at all. Not even a single young goat to have a party with my friends! But when this son of yours, who wasted all of your inheritance with prostitutes, comes back home, you kill the best young, fat nice-looking calf to feed him!"

The father answered, "Dear son, you have always lived with me and everything that I have is yours. But we must join in celebration and happiness together because your younger brother died already, but now he is living; he was lost but now I have found him again."

NOTES

NOTES

ABOUT THE AUTHOR

David Dale has traveled, lived and worked in Laos since 1997, where he has functioned in many different capacities, including a language student, an English teacher and a project manager for an agricultural development company. David married his wife, Malayvanh, in 2005 and along with their two children, they currently reside in the World Heritage city of Luang Prabang, where they operate two Saffron Espresso Caffès. David and Malayvanh have also established Saffron Coffee Company, <www.SaffronCoffee.com>, to promote Arabica coffee cultivation among disadvantaged mountain farmers and former growers of opium.

www.ingramcontent.com/pod-product-compliance
Lightning Source LLC
Chambersburg PA
CBHW060837190426
43197CB00040B/2663